HAUNTED INSIDE PASSAGE

Ghosts, Legends, and Mysteries
of Southeast Alaska

BJORN DIHLE

ALASKA
NORTHWEST
BOOKS®

Several chapters in this book have been previously published, often in different forms, in
newspapers and journals: "Naked Joe: Alaska's Most Famous and Least Known Ghost"
was published as "In the Spirit of Naked Joe" by *Earth Island Institute Magazine*; parts of
"The Mysteries of Yakobi Island" were published by the *Juneau Empire*; "The Legends of
Thomas Bay" was published in two different parts ("The Second Strangest Story"
and "More Strange Stories") by the *Capital City Weekly*; and "The Sinking of the Islander
and the Legend of Its Lost Gold" was published by the *Juneau Empire*.

Library of Congress Cataloging-in-Publication Data
Names: Dihle, Bjorn, author.
Title: Haunted Inside Passage : ghosts, legends, and tragedies of southeast
Alaska / Bjorn Dihle.
Description: Portland, Oregon : Alaska Northwest Books, 2017. | Includes
bibliographical references.
Identifiers: LCCN 2016034485 (print) | LCCN 2016039013 (ebook) | ISBN
9781943328949 (pbk.) | ISBN 9781943328956 (ebook)
Subjects: LCSH: Ghosts—Inside Passage. | Inside Passage—Folklore.
Classification: LCC BF1472.U6 D55 2017 (print) | LCC BF1472.U6 (ebook) |
DDC 133.109798/2—dc23
LC record available at https://lccn.loc.gov/2016034485

Designed by Vicki Knapton
Map by Robin Hanley and Alex Witt

Published by Alaska Northwest Books®
An imprint of

GRAPHIC ARTS
BOOKS®
P.O. Box 56118
Portland, Oregon 97238-6118
www.graphicartsbooks.com

CONTENTS

Preface 5

Acknowledgments 8

Map 9

1. The Mysteries of Yakobi Island 11

2. The Ghost of Castle Hill 23

3. A Testament to Ice 30

4. The Ghosts of Juneau's Past 36

5. The Terrible Fate of the SS *Clara Nevada* 46

6. The King Con of the Klondike 55

7. The Ghosts of Skagway 64

8. The Kóoshdaa Káa Chronicles 76

9. The Legends of Thomas Bay 100

10. The Sinking of the *Islander* and the Legend of Its Lost Gold 118

11. The Ghosts of the House of Wickersham 123

12. The Curious Case of
    "The Most Diabolical of Alaska's Murders" 129

13. The Tragedy of the *Princess Sophia* 141

14. Trouble with Bigfoot 150

15. The Witches of Southeast Alaska 166

16. It Came from the Depths: A Brief History of
    Southeast Alaska's Sea Monsters 176

17. The Haunting of the Mount Edgecumbe Hospital 187

18. The Ghosts of the Alaskan Hotel 194

19. Naked Joe: Alaska's Most Famous and Least Known Ghost 200

20. Juneau's Front Street Ghosts 204

Sources 213

PREFACE

DURING a hike on a mountain ridge above Juneau, my friend Ben offered me some advice on how to become a successful writer.

"You're never going to get anywhere unless you make it sexy. You need a book with big-breasted women and zombies," he said.

Maybe he was right. I looked east toward the edge of a 1,500-square-mile icefield, then west toward a wilderness archipelago full of brown bears. I tried the nature writer thing and the pile of rejection slips I received basically told me the same thing Ben was.

After our hike, while I was considering writing a nonfiction book about bondage among the undead, I received an unusual e-mail. A Juneau man named Carlton Smith had read a story I'd written about an investigation of a bay supposedly haunted by Kóoshdaa Káa, the boogeyman of Southeast Alaska, and wanted to meet. By the time we finished our first cup of coffee, Carlton suggested I write a book.

That night I fired off queries pitching a collection of Southeast Alaskan scary stories and unsolved mysteries to publishing companies.

I didn't hold back in my cover letter. I confessed that my golden retriever puppy, Fenrir, depressed by my failure as a writer, had taken to binge drinking toilet water. I made it clear my book could only be optioned into a film if Tom Hardy played me and Scarlett Johansson played my girlfriend, MC, an incredibly intelligent writer whose one flaw is that she's clumsy and burns herself whenever she tries to cook. I didn't expect to hear back, except for maybe a short note saying something like I was less funny than watching someone with hemorrhoids riding a bicycle across the country while being chased by a pack of rabid wiener dogs and Chihuahuas. Trust me—I've done it—it's not funny.

To my surprise, I had a book deal by the end of the week.

Haunted Inside Passage evolved into twenty different stories that each took on a life of its own. Reaching out and interviewing people who'd had supernatural and unexplainable experiences wasn't always easy. Despite being voted the "life of the party" senior year in high school, I'm intensely shy. Well, there was that time at my little brother's wedding in Newfoundland when I challenged the 300 or 400 Canadians at the reception to a tag-team wrestling match against me and the groom. (All I remember is yelling, "We will destroy you, Canada!" before my speech was prematurely ended.) Normally, I'm as introverted as a Bigfoot riding a unicorn being followed by a UFO. Luckily for me, most folks I reached out to seemed happy to tell me their stories. For some it was therapeutic. Only a few declined.

During the five months I invested in this book I worked nights in the mental health unit of a local hospital, often with extremely psychotic patients. During days and nights off, I wrote and obsessed over these stories. The irony is that, while I'm not much of a people person, I'm not much of a ghost guy either. I considered myself an open-minded skeptic. Partway into dozens of interviews, something in me began to change. The number of "normal" people who'd had eerie and unexplainable experiences was too great to not admit there was some truth to their stories and the legends. This book deals with some horrible events and terrifying themes. Some—the Kóoshdaa Káa for example—made me uncomfortable to explore and, even more so, to put on paper. A few times, I half wondered if "something" followed me home after an interview or tour of a supposedly haunted place.

I have to confess stories from the Canadian side of the Inside Passage, a little less than half of the nearly one-thousand-mile route, are few and far between in this book. That's not because Canadians aren't interesting or are lacking in spooky stories. I love Canada—even Quebec—but it would take another book to do the region justice. Who knows, perhaps someday there will be a sequel to *Haunted Inside Passage*.

For the maximum experience, read the following twenty stories in consecutive order. Some are fun, such as crusty fishermen who've tangled with sea monsters, my search for Sasquatch that ends in a casino, and the ghost of a nude survivalist with a zeal for publicity. Others will leave you wondering, such as the disappearance of fifteen sailors during first contact between Russians and Tlingits, the tales of the Kóoshdaa Káa haunting the rain forest, and the curious case of Alaska's first supposed serial killer. Some will break your heart, like the spirits of Mount Edgecumbe Hospital, or the sinking of the *Princess Sophia* and the ghosts of gold rush prostitutes said to still be at unrest. All in all, the book offers a window, for local and visitor alike, into the murky history of Southeast Alaska. Hopefully it will leave you haunted in a sexy sort of way.

Acknowledgments

A LOT of people helped with this book. Special thanks go to Carlton Smith for suggesting the project. Thanks also go to Joe and Sandy Craig for their friendship and stories; Peter Metcalfe for his advice and help with interviewing; Kathy Howard, my editor, for preventing me from looking even more of a fool; and my folks, Nils and Lynnette Dihle, for three decades of supporting me "coloring outside the lines." I'll never forget when I presented my dad with a draft of a "novel" I wrote when I was nineteen. It was so terrible he didn't know what to say, but he still offered encouragement. Special thanks also go to Mary Catharine Martin, the writer and adventurer with whom I share my life, for making me write again after a hiatus of nearly a decade. Her support and suggestions were critical to the creation of this book.

I'm grateful to the dozens of people who shared their stories and helped with my research: Nancy Strand, Frank Kaash Katasse, Ethel Lund, Nils Dihle, Dee Longenbaugh, Joshua Adams, Cori Giacomazzi, David Katzeek, Mike Stedman, Jake and Rachel Stedman, Teresa Busch, Elva Bontrager, Joe and Sandy Craig, Carlton Smith, Dennis Corrington, Renee Hughes, Steven Levi, J. Robert Alley, Brian Weed, Jesse Walker, Tara Neilson, Peter Metcalfe, and many more.

Thanks to the land, water, and people of Southeast Alaska. I hope these stories, testaments to the strange histories that have unfolded in the shadows of the rain forest, are enjoyed for generations to come.

Canada

Skagway

Lynn Canal

Cross Sound

Elfin Cove

Juneau

Yakobi Island

Tenakee Springs

Angoon

Thomas Bay

Petersburg

Sitka

Wrangell

N
W   E
S

Inside Passage

Ketchican

Alaska   CA

map location

1.

THE MYSTERIES OF
YAKOBI ISLAND

A T the southwest edge of Cross Sound lies Yakobi Island, a stormy rain forest shrouded in mystery. Originally named *Takhanes* by the Tlingit, it's located roughly eighty miles west of Juneau, near the small fishing communities of Elfin Cove and Pelican. It is much smaller, at roughly eighty-two square miles, than neighboring islands Chichagof, Admiralty, and Baranof. Part of the West Chichagof–Yakobi Wilderness, it seldom sees human visitors.

It was the summer of 2009, aboard the FV *Njord* with Joe and Sandy Craig, when I first saw the island. We were motoring across Cross Sound toward Elfin Cove after a morning pulling longline sets. The island's black forest towered into gray rain clouds. Waves crashed high on its cliffy shore. Halibut lay in blood and slime as Sandy and I baited hooks in the back while Joe sat at the helm.

"They think Yakobi is where Chirikov lost fifteen men," Sandy said, gesturing with a circle hook in her hand. "In Surge Bay, on the outer coast of the island, there's the remains of the lost Tlingit village of Apolosovo."

An entourage of seagulls followed, snatching up fish roe and guts from the ocean. On the mainland to the north, the white expanse of the Brady Icefield disappeared into the gray. A pod of humpback whales sounded, their fourteen-foot-wide tails barely visible in the far distance. I was too busy trying to keep up baiting hooks to offer more than an occasional grunt of curiosity as Sandy regaled me with stories. Once in a while I looked up and studied the froth of giant waves crashing against the island's rocky shore and felt a lonely sense of entrancement.

Yakobi haunted the periphery of my thoughts for much of the spring. What would it be like to hike through its maze of rain forest? What views would its mountains offer? What would I discover if I gave myself to the island? I had the suspicion it would swallow me if I ventured too deep. The island's history is eerie; some say it harbors one of Alaska's greatest unsolved mysteries.

In the summer of 1741, two Russian ships, the *St. Paul* and *St. Peter*, set sail from Avacha Bay on the Kamchatka Peninsula under the command of Vitus Bering. Aleksei Chirikov, captaining the *St. Paul*, lost sight of his commander's ship in foul weather early on in the crossing. He continued east, making it to the southern tip of what is known as Baranof Island on the 15th of July, a few days before Bering and his crew sighted land near Yakutat. For three days the *St. Paul* sailed north, giving the rugged coastline a wide berth, before reaching latitude 58 and sighting an inlet the captain believed offered a suitable landing. Many historians believe this inlet or bay to belong to Yakobi Island, likely Surge Bay or the southern entrance of Lisianski Strait. Chirikov, with the agreement of his officers, sent eleven men in a longboat to make a brief reconnaissance of the island and attain freshwater. The longboat rowed toward the dark forest and mountains, their captain on deck watching, before vanishing into the tapestry of the wilderness.

Longlining for halibut ended and trolling for salmon began. Spring turned to summer. Joe, Sandy, and I fished Surge Bay for the July king opener. The first morning the fish were coming aboard so fast I barely had time to take a break to vomit from being seasick. When the bite died, I looked up and stared at the dark ocean swells crashing on the black rocks surrounding the outer edge of the bay. The seas were placid, Joe told me—six feet was about as calm as it ever got. Much of the year ten foot and even bigger seas were common along the outer coast of the island. In late July, Joe and I chased sporadic schools of coho in Cross Sound. The fishing lulled. Thankfully, my skipper had good taste in literature—I read almost the entire canon of Knut Hamsun and Herman Hesse while waiting for fish to bite. One afternoon after a particularly slow day we anchored in Soapstone Cove of Yakobi Island, near the northern limit of Lisianski Strait.

"We lost money today," Joe said, shrugging. "Feel free to go for a hike."

I rowed an inflatable to shore, hauled it above high tide line, and pissed around it in hopes of discouraging bears from biting it. Following the shoreline, I entered a salt chuck with bear trails leading in every direction. The place seemed to scream that I wasn't welcome, but I ignored my inner Chicken Little and passed along the edge of a field of sedge and rye grass. A brown bear, brutally muscled, black on top and blond below, emerged from the forest forty yards away. Two cubs of the year somersaulted out behind and began wrestling with each other. Seeing me, the sow rose on her hind legs huffing, clacking her teeth, and debating whether or not to charge.

Two hundred and sixty-eight years before I encountered the bear, Aleksei Chirikov, eager for his men to return, sailed back and forth in front of the bay the longboat had entered. During the beginning of the wait, the captain wrote the weather was such "the longboat should have been able to come out to us freely. Later, heavy rains, fog, and strong winds arose and these winds carried us away from the bay for up to thirty minutes' distance."

After five days of pacing and worrying, a fire was sighted in the bay near where the longboat was last seen. The *St. Paul* fired a cannon numerous times to summon its estranged crew, but, despite the seas being calm, no boat came. After each time the cannon was fired,

Chirikov noted, the fire on the shore flared up. The captain and his crew, believing the longboat was damaged and the fire to be a signal asking for help, sent four men in their remaining dory to make repairs. Chirikov wrote, "We saw the boatswain in his dory approaching the shore about six o'clock after midday. However, he sent none of the signals that I instructed him to use and he did not return at the time expected, while the weather remained of the calmest."

Night came on and the captain, his nerves growing increasingly frayed, waited. The thoughts racing through his head can only be guessed. Perhaps he wondered what sort of land this was, where men just seem to vanish. In the gloom, as the *St. Paul* paced, the island loomed a deeper shade of darkness. One can imagine sleeplessness filled with dread and feelings of powerlessness. Perhaps the captain and crew whittled away the minutes squinting and straining their ears for the sound of a musket shot, voices, or the squeak and swoosh of oars. The next day, a little past noon, two boats came out of the bay where both of the missing parties of Russians had entered. At first the men aboard the *St. Paul* were elated, but it was soon apparent the boats were canoes— one was small, manned by four men, and the other, significantly larger, was paddled by many. The smaller approached within shouting distance and the Tlingits rose to their feet and according to Chirikov, "twice shouted 'Agai! Agai!' waving their arms." The canoes quickly turned and paddled for shore, ignoring Chirikov and his men as they waved white flags, bowed, and made other signs of friendliness in the hopes of attaining a meeting.

What the Tlingits were trying to tell the *St. Paul* has been much debated. Chirikov came to the conclusion the interaction was hostile. He wrote in his report to the Admiralty College: "It may be surmised, as the Americans did not dare approach our packet boat, that they had either treated our people onshore as enemies, and either killed or detained them."

Many locals, familiar with Surge Bay and the competency of Chirikov's seamanship, agree with the captain's conclusion. The best place to gather freshwater in the bay is in a narrow cove surrounded on both sides by cliffs, offering the perfect ambush. Peter Metcalfe, one of Joe Craig's best friends and the author of a number of books on Alaska Native history, is one of those people. He wrote the following in an e-mail:

> Having spent many days along the shores of West Yakobi in every manner of boat including kayak, canoe, various skiffs and other power craft up to commercial fishing vessels, I favor other possibilities (than currents capsizing and drowning the sailors). For two boats to founder days apart, you have to assume the men were rank amateurs and unable to pick up clues like kelp patches and disturbed swells. After all, they were not approaching the coast during a storm. I assume they were experienced boatmen who, at the first hint of danger, would alter their course. In the worst of conditions on West Yakobi, there is always a way through and into still water in the lee of the many islets. Sure there are currents, but if I could master them as a green kayaker, certainly a boat full of strong men at the oars could do even better. My conclusion is that the Tlingits present on that coast had something to do with the loss of the boats—either aiding a mutiny, which has been speculated but seems unlikely, or springing a surprise attack (more likely), or welcoming them to the shore, then taking the men captive (most likely).

However, other people believe the interaction was the opposite— that the Yakobi people were attempting to warn the *St. Paul* of vicious currents that likely capsized the two boats and led to the drowning of the fifteen Russians. The southwest entrance of Lisianski Strait and the entrance to Surge Bay can be dangerous at times, particularly when a westerly wind blows and the tide is ebbing. Allan Engstrom, who has written extensively about Russian history in Alaska, believes the two boats were lost to the perils of the sea. In his essay "Yakobi Island, the Lost Village of Apolosovo, and the Fate of the Chirikov Expedition," he states his belief that seas were running heavy from the west, that Chirikov miscalculated the distance his men were from the land, and that both ships were capsized in rough seas when they were out of the captain's view.

Chirikov waited another day and then, in agreement with his men, set sail for Avacha Bay on the twenty-seventh. With the loss of the *St. Paul's* two boats, they had no way to replenish their dwindling supply of freshwater. To wait any longer might compromise the lives of the entire crew. The 2,000-mile journey back was inglorious and brutal. With the shortage of freshwater and food, the sailors succumbed to scurvy and other illnesses. Chirikov never recovered from the voyage. He is remembered as a bold, intelligent, and compassionate explorer. His opinion and treatment of men, both his crew and indigenous people, was remarkably progressive. He died in debt at age forty-five from tuberculosis.

Nearly three centuries later, as I stood watching the bear froth at the mouth and huff, I thought about becoming disappeared. I slowly squatted, pumped a slug into the chamber of Joe's ancient shotgun, and tried to appear nonthreatening. Gradually she calmed and fell to all fours, but the hair on her hump remained standing as she began to cautiously nibble greens. Her two tiny cubs didn't share her agitation. One picked up a shell, sat, and rolled over on its back as its sibling pounced, perhaps at a small fish, in the water's shallows. I remained crouched and motionless. Very awkwardly, like a cramping tortoise attempting gymnastics, I tried to scoot-crawl away. The mother rose back to her full height, clacked her teeth, and swayed. She rushed forward a few steps, then stopped and stared back at her cubs. Slowly, she quieted, then fell to all fours and went back to nibbling on a patch of sedge. When her head was down and the cubs were wrestling, I made a quick getaway. Aboard the *Njord*, Joe and I made dinner. The ocean was calm and Three Hill Island rose into the fog. Joe gave me a hard time about my bear magnetism, mentioning something about bears being attracted to strong-smelling things like spawned-out salmon and rotten whales. That night as the boat gently rocked and the occasional breeze whistled through the trolling poles, I studied the dark forest of Yakobi Island. Somewhere nearby, the family of bears was looking for sustenance, or resting. I felt lucky for the encounter but also embarrassed. I'd ignored what the island was telling me, and it nearly led to violence. I put these thoughts aside and tried to fall asleep; we'd be hauling anchor before sunrise with the hope that the new tide would bring in a school of coho.

The mysteries of Yakobi Island do not end with the disappearance of Chirikov's men. In his essay about the lost village of Apolosovo, Engstrom also wrote of a vanished Tlingit village and how it might be connected with the fate of the Russian sailors. In 1805, Nikolai Rezanov, with the aid of Alexander Baranov, compiled a list of Tlingit villages. On Yakobi Island he noted "a village named Apolosovo or Vorovskoe by the Russians; in it the male inhabitants reach about 100." The village is never mentioned again after this report. Engstrom theorizes that Apolosovo, more isolated than other Tlingit villages, may have been more susceptible to the ravages of smallpox. Native Americans suffered horribly from old-world diseases, and Alaska Natives were no different. Some people theorize that 30 to 90 percent of the population died from these diseases. Ultimately, the speculation of what happened to Apolosovo remains as cloudy as what happened to the fifteen Russians.

Engstrom points out two uncanny links between Apolosovo and the Chirikov expedition. The first is an account recorded by Nathaniel Portlock, a fur trader anchored on the west side of Chichagof Island, in 1787. Portlock was struck by the difference in character between the Yakobi and other groups of Tlingits, noting the former were more warlike and dishonest, and that they made the other Tlingits uneasy. The Yakobi traders told a story that seemed to describe the events of Chirikov's second boat disappearing. Instead of capture or murder, they described a westerly wind, stormy seas, and desperate sailors fighting for their lives before capsizing and drowning.

The second link is an unusual petroglyph located in Surge Bay. Numerous depictions of salmon and halibut adorn rocks in the intertidal zone, but one petroglyph is quite different. Engstrom made the voyage to find it and described it in his essay as looking like a sailing ship and made much more recently. While the unusual petroglyph inspires more questions than answers, it is easy, for a moment, to imagine the people of the island looking out on the *St. Paul*.

The Craigs had lots of great stories: encounters with giant squids; a whale getting caught in their anchor line and hauling their boat out to sea; Raymond Lee, a mysterious recluse who sailed (and shipwrecked) all over the world; rogue waves on otherwise calm ocean. Through the years, bit by bit, they shared their own story. In 1971, when Joe was eighteen, he moved to Elfin Cove, close to the northern limit of Chichagof Island. He built a cabin, bought a small skiff, and hand trolled for salmon. At the end of his first season he didn't make enough money to cover gas and food. When I met him three and a half decades later, much of the Cross Sound fleet considered him one of their best king salmon fishermen. Sandy had hand trolled all over Southeast and homesteaded on Kupreanof Island until one fateful night at a bar in Juneau. The two young fishermen ran into each other and got to talking. The next thing Sandy knew, Joe had invited himself to spend the winter with her, cut off from the rest of the world, on Kupreanof Island. The beer must have been particularly good because Sandy agreed. More than any other story or legend, it was the mysteries of Yakobi Island we talked about the most. Each season we discussed going to search Surge Bay for the petroglyphs. Seven years passed. Something always came up to prevent us from making the journey. Finally, Sandy had enough.

"We're doing it. Don't even try arguing. You've never won an argument with me," she said one May while we were camped with my girlfriend, MC, and Cal, Joe and Sandy's son, in the Stikine River Delta.

In late June I met her in Elfin Cove. We ran up to the store to say hi to our friend JoAnn and grab a few last minute provisions—herring and beer—before heading out on the glassy waters of Cross Sound. The

Fairweather Mountains stood blurred and white in the seventy-degree heat wave. Joe was traveling with us in spirit. A year and a half prior we had spread his ashes on a mountain he loved. Memories flooded back as we passed Yakobi Rock and neared the rocky entrance of Surge Bay. How many of Joe's spreads did I lose overboard while trolling that first season, and then blame on pesky sea lions? Then there was that giant king that flopped off my gaff at Surge Bay while he was watching. There was no way I could blame a sea lion for that one.

"I'll never be able to forget that," he said sadly, and he never did. There was that bull killer whale that swam docilely with a pod of Dall porpoises. There was the humpback whale that spyhopped a sea otter six feet out of the ocean. There was the baby killer whale that almost touched the *Njord* one morning while we were pulling a halibut longline set. There was the big male bear that suddenly stood up ten feet away while I was sooty grouse hunting. There were conversations, about everything and anything, after long days of fishing.

Sea otters, murres, murrelets, and loons parted as Sandy slowly motored toward the rocky shore of Yakobi Island. Salmon milled and splashed, waiting for the right moment to move into freshwater and spawn. Bob-o Bell, a hard-core fisherman, banjo player, and explorer, paddled a kayak toward us after we threw anchor. Normally it would be a little surprising to happen upon someone alone out here, but seeing Bob-o felt oddly natural.

"Have you see Debra?" he asked, referring to his wife, also a commercial fishing captain. I shook my head. Having fished a couple commercial trolling king openers with her, I guessed she was busy riding a killer whale to Japan. Or maybe she'd commandeered a Chinese pirate ship. Kayaking the outer coast of Yakobi Island in such nice weather was likely just too easy for her.

After Sandy anchored, we rowed to shore and I tied our rapidly deflating raft to a cliff. We began meticulously searching different coves for the petroglyphs. I tried to imagine what it would be like to live here 274 years ago. How did the Takhanes people see this world?

What was it like for a giant ship to appear out on the big ocean and for strange men to row odd, small boats to their island? I couldn't help but think it had to be akin to experiencing a UFO landing and extraterrestrials trying to enter your home. A half hour later I scouted a beach that offered a good landing for canoes. Seeing nothing after a quick sweep, I noticed a petroglyph-covered boulder that seemed like a religious icon combined with a bulletin board. One, of a halibut, radiated most clearly. Others were of salmon, circles, swirls, and the head of an eagle or thunderbird.

"Five times I've tried to find these petroglyphs," Sandy said quietly as she sat on a rock and studied the marks of the ancients. At the northern edge of the cove, I happened upon the petroglyph of the supposed two-masted ship on a gray rock. We studied it carefully—its hull was much deeper than a canoe. It had four oars, a bowsprit, two ovals mid-ship that could be interpreted as sails, an oval atop the stern, and what appeared to be an anchor line. Sandy came to a conclusion faster than I did.

"I think this has to be the second, smaller boat Chirikov lost. The four oars must mean four men and it kind of looks like what others have called sails could actually be men," Sandy said. I agreed, but also wondered if the carving was a depiction of a conglomeration of the *St. Paul* and the smaller boats. This was the likely site of first contact between two worlds. This was where what many call the greatest mystery in Alaska occurred. Perhaps this was the place where a village "containing a hundred men" once stood. Whether the fifteen explorers drowned, were murdered, or captured, I could only guess. What struck me most was how small, fragile, and barely visible these images were in relation to the rain forest and ocean. It had been more than 200 years since the Takhanes people had disappeared. The severe weather and hungry rain forest had helped the earth absorb all signs of habitation.

We hauled anchor, picking our way between rocks and out onto the big ocean to fish a few hours of the evening tide. The outer coast of Yakobi Island generally teems with fish in late June, so we were surprised after an hour of trolling without even a humpy to show for our efforts. At tide change, a rod began to hammer and line zinged out. Sandy hooted and hollered as I played the king. Its dark back glittered as it sliced through the clear water. We added a fat coho to the ice chest before heading into Surge Bay to anchor for the night. Dawn came sunny and calm; a storm was supposed to roll in late in the day, so we hurried out to fish the morning. Sandy had recently bought her little boat in Juneau. Though it rode well and had character, it tended to break down frequently. Sandy was adept at fixing it, but there were a thousand things we'd rather do than fight with a rebellious engine in stormy seas. A pole began hammering soon after we got our gear down. After landing the king, we added a handful of fat coho to the cooler. (Sandy was planning on smoking the majority of them. Her smoked fish is some of the best in northern Southeast.) The last king of the morning was a hog. The rain forest mountains of Yakobi Island glowed in the dawn on one side and a wilderness of glaciers and mountains shone on the other.

In the early afternoon, we motored away from Yakobi Island. The wind began to pick up as we passed into Elfin Cove's inner harbor. We visited with a few friends and grabbed a couple of things from Joe and Sandy's old house. That night, at the Craigs' cabin in Gull Cove, we opened a bottle of whiskey and toasted the ghosts of the Chirikov expedition, the lost village of Apolosovo, and the folks we've loved and lost. A humpback whale lunge-fed in the still waters nearby.

We spent the morning halibut fishing and pulling shrimp pots in Icy Strait. After a couple hours we had three twenty-five-pounders, my favorite size for eating, and a few dinners' worth of prawns. We processed the fish, vacuum packing some and getting a load in a brine to be smoked. At Elfin Cove, I said good-bye to Sandy and then begged a ride on a Beaver floatplane full of sports fishermen who'd fly to Juneau and then return to their lives in big cities down south. I glanced back at Cross Sound—it was covered in rain clouds, and the ocean was full of whitecaps. Clouds swirled and parted to reveal green mountains. We

Poe, painted hours after her death, depicts a beautiful, pale, voluptuous girl with her head turned to the side like she'd gracefully accepted her fate. Less than two years later Edgar was found on a park bench raving. He died from unknown causes shortly after.

A lot of well-known Southeast Alaskan ghost stories involve youngish women who died wronged by fate or a man—in some cases, both. Many believers and skeptics of the supernatural are leery. Dee Longenbaugh, historian and owner of Observatory Books, thinks most Southeast ghost stories are exaggerations or never happened. For a bibliophile, there could be no finer death than being caught in the Observatory during an earthquake—I've never been in a place so claustrophobic with books and maps.

Dee thinks spooky stories that are more likely true often don't seem to have a point. (Joshua Adams, son of the owners of the famous and haunted Alaskan Hotel and an adamant believer in ghosts, feels similarly. He cautioned me about getting lost in the glamour of ghostly legends and claimed the "real stories are a little monotone.") Dee possesses a deep knowledge of Russian Alaskan history, a history that's often buried and misconstrued. She moved to Mount Edgecumbe on Japonski Island in 1963. Her husband was the new chief of surgery at the hospital. A few years later the couple made the quarter-mile move to Sitka, a thriving arts, science, and cultural mecca on Baranof Island.

Sitka acts as the setting for the most famous Southeast ghost story that predates the Klondike gold rush. Castle Hill, rising above downtown, is said to be haunted by the ghost of a Russian princess. She's been called "the Lady in Blue" or "Black" or "White" depending on which story you hear. Maybe, like a lot of princesses, she's too fashionably complex to be limited to just one outfit. My exposure to Russian princesses, and Russian culture for the matter, is pitifully limited, though I once found myself in a rather odd scenario with a vodka czar, his war criminal buddies, and a bunch of prostitutes. My closest encounter with Russian princesses happened while hanging out with my lovelorn friend Ben. One night a group of Russian exchange students were gathered outside a university dance. I was exhausted from several hours of driving around with Ben, listening to sad music, going from bar to bar, and attempting awkward conversations with anyone female.

"We have to talk to them!" Ben yelled, gesturing at the girls a few yards away. "I'm not leaving until we talk to them!"

"They can hear us," I said.

"It doesn't matter! They don't even speak English!" he yelled.

"Well, go talk to them."

"I'm not talking to them."

"What?"

"You talk to them," Ben said. We argued for several minutes while the girls grew increasingly nervous. Wearing leather, fur, and lots of makeup, they were obviously way out of our league. The last thing on earth I wanted to do was attempt conversation, but Ben's resolution appeared unbreakable. I lowered my head to avoid eye contact, stumbled toward the girl who looked the least likely to have ties to the KGB, and stuttered the best Russian pickup line I could think of.

"So . . . so . . . who . . . who . . . do . . . do you prefer, Dostoyevsky or Tolstoy . . . Tolstoy?" I asked, then laughed, maybe a little too hysterically. Ben paced in the background, glaring with hormonal fury. Seconds passed like hours before the girl answered in a thick accent, "You tell me."

This was followed by tense moments of silence that felt like having your head on a chopping block and waiting for the ax to fall. I looked off into space as hard as I could. Finally, she put me out of my misery. "Our boyfriends are coming soon."

"Wow," Ben said as we drove away, blasting sad music. "Man, you were so rejected."

Perhaps because of my humiliating interaction with these Russian women, I was biased in my approach to the story of the Castle Hill haunting. It seemed too romantically formulaic to take seriously. The whole princess thing was annoying. I even considered not writing the story up, but it's not my job to censor the past. Often times the fictions we tell ourselves—no matter how ridiculous they might seem—are equally as vital as the truths we ignore.

The story begins with the founding of Sitka, one of the most beautiful and interesting small cities in North America. Situated at the ramparts of the rugged mountains of Baranof Island and looking out toward the big ocean, it's considered the second capital of Alaska. Kodiak was first. The Shee Atika' Tlingit were the masters of the area, including the sea otter pelt trade, when Alexander Baranov showed up with his fleet of Aleut hunters in 1799 to try to establish the small settlement, New Archangel, nearby. The Tlingit attacked the fort and massacred its inhabitants in 1802. Two years later, Baranov returned with a flotilla of nearly 1,000 men, mostly Aleut hunters. Before attempting to reestablish New Archangel, Baranov paraded his force through much of Southeast Alaska to strike fear and respect into the different Tlingit clans. In late September of 1804, after a series of failed negotiations and hostilities, the Russian began bombarding the Tlingit fort near Indian River just outside of where downtown Sitka stands today. After several days, and many casualties on both sides, the Tlingit made a long and difficult exodus through the woods and mountains to the other side of the island.

A cloud of controversy and, at least on my part, almost disbelief surrounds Alexander Baranov. How did a humble Russian merchant who, supposedly largely out of boredom, decided to try his hand in the Siberian fur trade and became bankrupt after an attack by Chukchi Natives, end up, mostly by his own devices, building a Russian Empire in Alaska? He was in his mid-forties when he signed on to the Russian-American Company. He never saw his country or Russian family again. The twenty-eight years he spent securing a foothold for Russia and dominating the fur trade were filled with adventure, violence, and dramatic cultural change. Aleut hunters employed by the company traveled all the way down to California in search of sea otters. Baranov married a Kenai Native and had two children, to whom he was reportedly a good father and for whom he had much affection. Shortly before he was

admit that writing about the ghost of a Russian princess haunting a castle had been kind of fun in a fairy-tale sort of way. It felt like a break from the madness my life mostly consisted of that winter. I'm not complaining, but spending days engrossed in Southeast's supernatural history and then working nights at a hospital with people suffering from acute psychosis was a little weird and heavy at times. I was on the verge of writing a cute and witty ending, something along the lines of the arrival of a ghost prince and how the princess was even more miserable after a few years of cohabitation, when I made the grave mistake of Googling "Castle Hill, Sitka." An image of the building burning popped up with a little story in the caption below. The fire occurred March 27, 1894, at two o'clock in the morning. No one knows how the blaze began. The only person residing in the building, a man who'd been asleep, barely escaped. I stared at the old photo and something struck me as odd. I blew the image up as big as it could go before I saw "it" standing in the window.

"MC," I said, passing her my laptop. "What do you see in the window below and just to the right of the lighthouse?"

"Oh, God!" she said, and shoved my computer back at me. "It looks like the silhouette of a person surrounded by flames."

We both knew about apophenia—seeing meaningful patterns in random data—and if I hadn't been looking for something eerie, I doubt I would have thought twice about the human-looking shape standing in the window. In all likelihood, it's nothing. At least that's what I told myself as I drove to work, no longer so sure that the haunting of Castle Hill was just a silly fairy tale.

3.

A Testament

to Ice

I N 1898, more than 3,000 gold rush stampeders attempted to trek from the Gulf of Alaska over the Valdez Glacier. Their plan was to reach the northern terminus of the glacier, and then travel hundreds of miles through the northern wilderness to the Klondike goldfields in the interior of the Yukon. They'd been tricked by shipping companies who told them the journey was shorter and easier than the more popular overland routes from Skagway and Dyea in northern Southeast Alaska. Most had never seen a glacier, let alone attempted to shuttle backbreaking loads of gear and food across a labyrinth of ice. After months of agonizing work, nearly all of the men and the handful of women were battered and dejected. There they spent a miserable winter, starving, diseased, and suffering from scurvy. Legend has it that more than a thousand died. Stranger still, many survivors believed a demon lived on the glacier and was responsible for a lot of the deaths.

The tragedy might have been entirely forgotten if Captain W. R. Abercrombie hadn't arrived on the scene in April of 1899. His account of the Valdez route was published in *Alaska. 1899. Copper River*

Exploring Expedition. He describes never before having seen such a motley and desperate-looking group of people as the group of stampeders camped in Valdez. Many of the men he'd met the year before but didn't recognize due to their changed appearances. The quartermaster's agent, Charles Brown, reported, "My God, Captain, it has been clear hell! I tell you the early days of Montana were not a marker to what I have gone through this winter! It was awful!"

When Abercrombie visited the cabins that "housed some 80 or 100 of these destitute prospectors" he saw that Brown had not been exaggerating. The dwellings smelled of decay, rot, disease, and death. Abercrombie wrote

> They were crowded together, from 15 to 20 in log cabins, 12 by 15, and in the center of which was a stove. . . . Most of them were more or less afflicted with scurvy, while a few of them had frost-bitten hands, faces and feet. . . . I noticed in talking to these people that over 70 percent of them were more or less mentally deranged. My attention was first directed to this fact by their reference to a 'glacial demon.' One big, raw-boned Swede, in particular, described to me how this demon had strangled his son on the glacier, his story being that he had just started from Twelve-Mile Plant (a small collection of huts just across the Coast Range of Mountains from Valdez) with his son to go to the coast in company with some other prospectors. When halfway up the summit of the glacier, his son, who was ahead of him hauling a sled, while he was behind pushing, called to him, saying that the demon had attacked him and had his arms around his neck. The father ran to his son's assistance, but, as he described it, his son being very strong, soon drove the demon away and they passed on their way up towards the summit of Valdez Glacier. The weather was very cold and wind blowing very hard, so that it made traveling very difficult in passing over the ice between the huge

crevasses through which it was necessary to pick their way to gain the summit. While in the thickest of these crevasses, the demon again appeared. He was said to be a small, heavy-built man and very active. He again sprang on the son's shoulders, this time with such a grasp that, although the father did all he could to release him, the demon finally strangled the son to death. The old man then put the son on the sled and brought him down to Twelve-Mile camp, where other prospectors helped him bury him.

During the recital of this tale the old man's eyes would blaze and he would go through all the actions to illustrate just how he fought off this imaginary demon. When I heard this story there were some ten or twelve other men in the cabin and at that time it would not have been safe to dispute the theory of the existence of this demon on the Valdez Glacier, as every man in there firmly believed it to be a reality.

I was informed by Mr. Brown that this was a common form of mental derangement incident to those whom a fear of scurvy had driven out over the glacier, where so many had perished by freezing to death.

One hundred and eight winters later, with my friend Mike Janes, I skied blindly through a blizzard across the upper reaches of the Llewellyn Glacier. We'd come up with the bright idea of traversing the Juneau Icefield—a conglomeration of 1,500 square miles of glaciers and mountains—in early February. There was a certain overprivileged, REI yuppie type of madness to our endeavor. This world of ice challenged my sense of space, time, and reality so much that I felt a kinship to the prospectors marooned on the Valdez Glacier. More worrisome, I was also beginning to feel a strange affinity for the supposed glacier demon. I'm hairy, smell bad, have funny teeth, and possess antisocial tendencies. A heavy gust of wind nearly knocked me over, a reminder that there were more pressing matters to consider, like whether or not we were staying the right course toward Atlin Lake. Toward dusk, I got a feeling something bad was nearby.

"Something isn't right," I yelled, bracing against the wind. Gradually I made out the sinister outline of a serac—a jagged protrusion of ice that meant nothing but pain and sorrow. I tossed a snowball ahead and it disappeared into a white abyss.

"Dammit," I yelled as Mike coiled up the slack in the rope connecting the two of us. "I led us right into the middle of an icefall."

The swirling gray dimmed as we, afraid to travel any farther, dug a snow shelter and pitched our tent. After dinner, I stared up into the darkness, listened to the storm, and thought about glaciers. They're challenging and otherworldly, move like a living thing, break open with yawning crevasses, and jumble into treacherous icefalls. Glaciers can inspire a visceral dread. I felt like a self-sentenced criminal, imprisoned in the Pleistocene Epoch. Before dawn, I crawled out of my cocoon and was buffeted by winds as I studied the nebulous world. A ground blizzard raged, but the clouds had vanished to reveal towering mountains and a canopy of stars. An eerie expanse of white seracs, blue where the wind had exposed the ice, surrounded us. We made coffee and broke camp as mountains slowly came to life with the flush of dawn. What had felt nightmarish the evening before turned into a vista fit for a dream. By dusk we made it near the top of the last icefall, which spilled like a frozen waterfall to the earth below. Staring out at the distant white of Atlin Lake surrounded by the dark blur of taiga, I thought of glaciers not as desolate geographic features, but instead as titans that created and destroyed the world.

The recent history of Southeast Alaska, and of much of the Northern Hemisphere, begins with ice. Mountains of ice. Oceans of ice. Continents of ice. So much ice that sea levels around the world were hundreds of meters lower than they are today. Nearly all of Southeast Alaska was locked in the solitude of ice until around 11,000 years ago, when the earth's temperatures rose dramatically. The glaciers rapidly melted, carved fjords, mountains, and valleys, and created lakes and rivers. Soon after, animals and people migrated in. They molded their lives from the land, glaciers, and ocean.

In the morning we edged along the spilling icefall until we down-climbed onto the flank of a mountain. Stunted willows and alders, the pioneer plants, began to appear. Trudging across land felt surreal; neither of us fully trusted that we no longer had to worry about falling into crevasses. In the fading twilight, as alpenglow reddened the mountains, I stared at the Llewellyn Glacier winding up into the icefield. Its appearance and brutality were deceptive. The gigantic mass of ice is considered to be the source of the Yukon River, which stretches all the way to the Bering Sea and is the lifeblood of the Yukon and Alaska. Many Athabascan people at least used to believe the headwaters of the Yukon was where spirits of the dead went to reside. Glaciers created much of the world and they also, in their way, nourish it. Southeast Alaska's rich marine and terrestrial biodiversity owes much to the carbon, sediment, and freshwater contributed by glaciers.

Our destination was the small community of Atlin, founded during the Klondike by prospectors in 1898. The town is located fifty-some miles from the terminus of the Llewellyn Glacier—Atlin Lake is nearly 500 square miles. We skied across overflow, growing increasingly nervous we'd break through as temperatures warmed and rain began to fall. Slush weighed down our skis and even clung to our sleds. In the dark we made it to a tiny islet, dug out a meter of saturated snow, and camped on land. The following night, after giving up on our useless skis and hauling them atop our sleds, we made it to the eastern shore of the lake. At the Atlin Inn, a number of Austrians wearing inordinately tight pants, suspenders, and sunglasses studied us from the shadows.

"How was the snow?" asked a guy who looked like Bono's doppelganger. He sounded a little desperate. It quickly became apparent they'd spent thousands of dollars traveling here to go heli-skiing.

"Mountains around here look pretty wind blasted," I said, trying to sound sympathetic.

"You guys were skiing where?" he asked.

"From Juneau, over the icefield," I said making the motion of cross-country skiing that he must have interpreted as a dance. He grabbed his suspenders and began a strange caper like a chicken hopping around looking for insects. I wished him good luck, sidled up to the bar next to Mike, and asked for a beer. A friendly blond girl filled a pint, then looked over at the Austrians and remarked, "Those guys sure like to party. They drank all our tequila last night. In a few hours they'll start blasting techno music and things are going to get really weird."

We ordered one more round and called it a night. It took us three days to hitchhike the 150 miles to Skagway. We caught a ride with two good ol' truckers hauling cars from Whitehorse to the coast. At the US border, the customs officer couldn't believe we'd traversed the icefield.

"Did you see any bears up there? Are you going to write a book about it?" he asked. I shook my head. He asked Mike if he found any bales of pot up on the glaciers. Mike shook his head. "All right, have a great day!"

The wind howled off the Juneau Icefield and the seas roiled in a mess of whitecaps as we rode the ferry down Lynn Canal, one of the longest and deepest fjords in the world. It too existed only because of the will and movements of a glacier. From the warmth of the observatory lounge, I thought of those men and women who suffered and died on the Valdez Glacier a century before. They'd hoped for riches but instead, those who survived returned south broken, destitute, and confounded. How long were they haunted by nightmares of ice demons and glaciers? The ferry bucked and shuddered in the frothing waves. I closed my eyes and saw a beautiful, unattainable, and lonely expanse of glaciers. Creator or destroyer—either way, Southeast Alaska is a testament to ice.

4.

The Ghosts
of Juneau's Past

ON a dark December day, I walked with my golden retriever, Fenrir, past the ruins of the Treadwell Mine. Still a puppy, "Fen" chased seagulls in the ocean's surf while I moped along behind. My girlfriend, MC, and I named her after the wolf in Norse mythology that killed Odin and destroyed the world. Her aptitude for apocalyptic behavior had proved low thus far, though she occasionally jumped on frightened strangers to lick them and drank voraciously from the toilet no matter how hard we tried to discipline her. MC was the bad cop and I was the pushover in our dog rearing. I used to be tough and mean, but with Fen I just found all her antics—even crappy water drinking—endearing. We live on Douglas Island, above Sandy Beach, where the mine boomed in the late 1800s and busted in the early 1900s. During its thirty-five-year life it was the largest hard rock mining operation in the world, and extremely dangerous to work in. Some say that on average a death occurred each day. There's no way to know the count for sure. There's speculation that many, if not most, of the deaths weren't recorded; estimates of the numbers are anywhere from fewer than 200 to more than 6,000. Near the Treadwell ruins, a Tlingit village—where people were living—was razed in the 1960s to make room for a boat harbor and ball fields. Pipes, decaying concrete, and a variety of rusted and bent chunks of steel, now considered historical artifacts, checkered the beach and forest. Two ravens followed a woman dressed in all black, walking a dog and beelining toward us.

"We don't wants to talk to her," I grumbled. "Curse it and crush it! We hates it forever!" During winter in Southeast Alaska I frequently turn into a more introverted, chubby version of Gollum from *The Lord of the Rings*. Besides, there was something eerie about this raven woman. Perhaps, she was a witch? I thought of a student named Nick, who was studying "birds and shit," in a college backpacking class I teach, who was obsessed with the Blair Witch. From my perspective it was only a scary movie, but Nick, who'd recently gotten out of a rough relationship, was adamant it was real. He planned to travel to Maryland and search the woods until he found her. More than morbidly fascinated, Nick wanted to do it out of a desperate belief that the power of love can conquer all. Through patience and persistence he hoped to teach the witch how to laugh, love, and enjoy food other than small children. I felt this raven lady might be an adequate substitute for the Blair Witch, so I let her catch up so I could snag her digits for Nick.

"Hey, can we walk our dogs together?" she asked. "Hello? You okay?"

"Sure," I said after a minute of staring and wondering whether she'd sink or float if I bound and threw her into the ocean. She talked of dogs and small things, and I occasionally grunted or moaned in affirmation. Finally, I had to ask.

"How do you feel about children?"

"What? I prefer dogs."

"Do you believe in the power of love?" She gave me a weird look. "That's too bad. I thought there was hope for you. On second thought, there's always hope. Can I get your number?"

After a tense parting with the raven woman, Fen and I skirted the edge of the "glory hole," where a cave-in in 1917 meant the death of Treadwell. The mine's wooden structures burned down in the 1920s, but a handful of spooky concrete buildings covered in moss and graffiti remained. It would be the perfect place to shoot a horror movie, maybe a flick about a young ornithologist looking for love in all the wrong places. I walked into the office building and studied the chaos of graffiti, mold, and moss. Just outside the entry, Fenrir paced and barked, something she almost never does. The artwork was unusual. Thank goodness there was none of that "John and Sally Forever" and cartoon people with penises for noses sort of nonsense. Rather, it appeared a horde of lunatics were given cans of spray paint, zapped with cattle rods, and told that if they didn't express themselves the world was going to end.

"All right, princess," I said, stepping outside. Fen tried to leap into my arms. Even though she was six months old and forty pounds, when she got scared she preferred to be carried. I wouldn't indulge her fears, so she rammed my leg with her head as we walked to an empty playground. I looked back into the wind and rain, out onto Gastineau Channel, which stretched into a gray wilderness. The city of Juneau clung to a mountain on the other side of the channel. I could barely see the vestiges of the AJ Mine etched out in the wintry forest.

The most accepted version of the founding of Douglas and Juneau reads like a dark comedy. In 1880 George Pilz, one of the first professional mining engineers in Alaska, based out of Sitka, was grubstaking prospectors. Pilz, remembered as a bitter and potentially unreliable narrator, was said to have offered 100 Hudson's Bay wool blankets to any Tlingit who brought him good information that led to a strike. The story goes that hearing this, the shaman Chief Kowee of the Auk Kwaan, whose territory included Gastineau Channel, canoed to Sitka with a rich sample of ore. Pilz sent Joe Juneau and Richard Harris, broke prospectors who'd recently been mining in Cassiar, British Columbia, to investigate. Supposedly, Juneau and Harris focused more on trading their outfit for hooch (Tlingit-made hard alcohol) and the favors of women than looking for gold. The dynamic duo, drunk and asleep, lost

Pilz's canoe to the rising tide before heading back to Sitka with not much more than a couple of hangovers and a borrowed boat. Chief Kowee returned to Sitka to plead with Pilz for another chance, and then dragged Juneau and Harris back. He took them up a creek and basically rubbed their faces in gold. After acquiring around 1,000 pounds of high-grade ore, Juneau and Harris apparently conspired to go for a long "recreational" paddle to Wrangell and then planned to enjoy a cruise south aboard a steamer. Another miner, working a claim near Holkham Bay where Juneau and Harris stopped by, encouraged the two at gunpoint to return to Sitka and report to Pilz.

David Katzeek, whose Tlingit name is Kingeisti, an elder and leader of the Eagle Thunderbird Clan of Klukwan, tells a different story about how Juneau came to be. The Auk Kwaan were leery of Juneau and Harris when they showed up in their canoe in Gastineau Channel and refused to let them land onshore even though they were starving. Finally, the Tlingit women, after conferring amongst themselves, approached their men and told them, "These are precious human beings like us. You can't treat them any less than ourselves." The men went out and asked the two prospectors to share their food, shelter, and gold. According to David, the Auk Kwaan men wore ammo belts that carried bullets made of gold, and that's where the name "Juneau Gold Belt," used to describe a roughly 100-mile region, comes from.

Regardless of how Juneau, Harris, and Kowee interacted and found gold, the find started a stampede and a township. In less than a year the entire Gold Creek Valley was filled with miners working all available claims. There was bitterness amongst the players most responsible in the founding of Juneau. Joe Juneau spent much of the first winter drinking, facilitating the inebriation of other miners, and chasing young female members of the Auk Kwaan. He bought enough people drinks to have the township named after him, even though Harris had claimed the title for himself. Ever the drifter, Juneau rambled on in 1882, leaving behind a pregnant teenager. He died in Dawson City in 1899, just as the Klondike gold rush was petering out. Richard Harris didn't go out of his way to make friends. All his claims were taken from him and he died broke from tuberculous in a sanitarium in Arizona. Pilz chased minerals from one tip of the world to the other, and died an ornery codger in Eagle in 1926. Chief Kowee supposedly never received the 100 promised blankets. During his wake in 1892, it was said he asked to be dressed for two days in his police uniform for his white friends and dressed in Tlingit regalia for two days for Native mourners before being cremated.

Shortly after gold was discovered in Juneau the constant pounding of stamp mills crushing ore overwhelmed Gastineau Channel. Douglas Island, Treadwell City, and Douglas City—more populous than Juneau during the first few decades—were laid out in several different factions, depending on race and, in cases like prostitution, trades. It might be an understatement to say that life was rough and tense at times. Historian Robert Campbell noted that, "For several years at the Juneau mines, mine owners pitted one working population against another, with the Treadwell workers—mostly immigrant Europeans and Tlingit—losing their position to what one contemporary called derisively 'the Chinese two-legged machines.' . . . Bringing Chinese workers up from the south, the mine owners hoped to break the mine workers' ability to dictate the conditions of their labor and their wages. 'The miners were,' according to one visitor, 'most of them foreigners and Indians, which partly took the curse of never ending accidents.'"

Anti-Chinese sentiment was strong throughout the West. It reached its apex in Juneau and Douglas in 1885 and 1886. Historian Earl Redman tells of a series of Chinese homes dynamited by angry white miners. The madness culminated on August 6, 1886. Redman writes, "A group of 105 men from Juneau crossed to Douglas. The mob dragged 60 Chinese workers from the mill, another 20 from their homes, collected 7 more from Juneau, then packed them onto two small ships, the schooner *Nellie Martin* and the sloop *Charlie*. With nothing but the clothes they wore, the Chinese men were sent sailing down Gastineau Channel. The two small ships eventually returned to Juneau, but the 87 Chinese refugees were never heard of again. Little was done to find them or to prosecute the bigoted mob leaders."

Fen and I climbed the wonky set of stairs to St. Ann's Avenue. She knew we were nearing our condo and she would soon be able to lie on her spot on the couch—or anywhere, for the matter, since she ruled the house—and was feeling good about life again. Most buildings in our neighborhood were constructed atop the rubble of Treadwell City and a variety of cemeteries, including Taku Tlingit burial grounds. There are stories of ghosts in several buildings. Russell Gilchriest, who used to work in the nearby Gastineau Elementary as a gym supervisor, told me of being "totally creeped out" while closing the gym down one evening. He was alone when doors began slamming and he heard the sound of something being dragged across the gym floor. The air suddenly got cold, even though all the windows were shut. Gilchriest, who hasn't had any other spooky experiences, said two or three Gastineau School coworkers had similar things happen. There are other stories, too. The sound of footsteps made by an invisible presence through apartments. Apparitions in the ruins of the Treadwell Mine. Boot prints in Sandy Beach that suddenly just disappeared.

The bluster was dying as Fen and I drove over the bridge to Juneau to interview Renee Hughes, who, along with her husband, cares for the Last Chance Mining Museum. Fresh snow clung to Mount Juneau and Mount Roberts, the sentry peaks guarding the Gold Creek Basin. The high school and numerous houses were built under one of Mount Juneau's huge slide paths which, according to many mountain experts, is one of the biggest urban avalanche disasters waiting to happen. Many of the homes and buildings in the area were built on mine tailings. With high-grade ore gone and operations, for the most part, long abandoned, many folks forget the herculean effort and madness that went into mining the Juneau area. To say that prospectors combed nearly every inch of Southeast's wilderness with a fine-toothed comb is only a slight exaggeration. Many entrances to mine adits have caved in or become overgrown by the rain forest. At one time Spalding

Meadows, a plateau covered with muskegs, had more than sixty claims being worked. Today, only Greens Creek Mine on northern Admiralty Island and the Kensington Mine in Berners Bay remain operating in the Juneau area.

Nestled in the shadow of Lion's Head Mountain, Kensington Mine has had men working it off and on since the Klondike gold rush. Jesse Walker, an employee and a grizzly bear of a man, is leery of all things supernatural but began having odd experiences at the remote mining camp.

"I am skeptical, but there is definitely something weird in the warehouse," he told me. The warehouse was built quite recently but it's located near or on the Jualin mining camp that operated from 1896 to 1928. Archaeologists combed the area and collected artifacts that now "are stored upstairs in the mezzanine in the warehouse." On four or five occasions while Jesse has been alone in the building, working in his downstairs office at night, he's heard a chair roll across the floor upstairs. Each time he went upstairs, turned on the lights, and found nobody there. One employee, whom Jesse described as "kind of a ghost hunter," was alone in the warehouse one night waiting to receive freight. He felt a presence and began taking pictures. According to Jesse, one of the images shows a ghostly face staring down from the mezzanine. Often the lights will turn off and on inexplicably. Around ten people have admitted to having experiences. On one occasion, the story goes, two miners were so frightened by something they refused to go back into the building as long as they worked at Kensington. Jesse doesn't get the feeling the ghost is malicious, though.

"I think he's probably more just checking out what we're doing. He's probably really impressed with computers and shit," Jesse said.

Brian Weed, a local explorer and mining history enthusiast, has walked and mapped many of the forgotten mines in the area surrounding Juneau. A friend of Brian's once confessed to a rather odd experience while exploring the AJ Mine in the 1970s when he was a teenager. He and a number of friends were on level four of the Hall Tunnel when the man veered off on his own to check out a side adit. He found a break room covered in "polar bear" mold, a six- to nine-inch fungus that looks like the hair of a polar bear. There were playing cards on the table, coats hanging on the wall, and other odd signs. He retraced his path back to the main tunnel, found his friends, and told them they had to see the room. He looked and looked but couldn't, try as he might, find the adit that led to the mysterious break room.

Fen and I turned onto Gold Street, climbed to Basin Road, and drove over an old wooden bridge clinging to a gorge. This was the first road constructed in Alaska and once serviced a multitude of mining operations, some of which were the largest gold producers in the world during their time. One of the more pleasant strolls in Juneau is the Perseverance Trail, which begins at the end of Basin Road. The hike ends in Silver Bow Basin, which according to author Willette Janes, "once boasted . . . a mess hall that could seat 500 men." It's hard to imagine the bustle that once existed. Now, the alder-filled valley and mountains are silent save for the wind and cascading streams.

"I'll be back soon," I told Fen at the Mount Roberts Trailhead. Every November, the last mile of road is gated off due to avalanche danger. The Last Chance Mining Museum, once the Alaska Juneau Gold Mining Company's compressor building, is about a half-mile walk. Renee and her husband live there year-round. The last light of the day was turning a darker shade of gray as I crossed the footbridge over Gold Creek. The mountains above looked desolate and brutal; this was the perfect setting for a sequel to the movie *The Shining*. A Great Pyrenees mountain dog barked and eyed me skeptically for a few moments before nestling its huge head into my side to be petted.

"Hello?" I called into the huge, dimly lit room full of mining artifacts, including one of the largest air compressors in the world. Renee emerged from a shadowy office above, walked down the stairs, and said hello. There have long been rumors the Gold Creek Valley is haunted. Renee is sure it is. Originally from Louisiana, she moved to Juneau in 1991 and immediately began caretaking the museum.

"I truly believe that there are ghosts here," Renee said. "There were so many people that came up here looking for gold, that it was such a passion during their life that they couldn't give up."

She's never seen a ghost, but frequently hears them talking to each other and laughing. "The other day I heard them laughing. It's three o'clock in the morning and I hear these two laughing out right behind my window. I know there's nobody back there because she [her dog] would have gone bonkers. I have had one volunteer, he was up here for a long time, that saw one. Some guy in an old miner's jacket and old hat looking in the window. He immediately went outside and the guy was nowhere to be found. He looked and looked and looked and couldn't find him. Then Floyd [another employee], he was actually underground. He knew he was the only one supposed to be underground that day. He was in the Perseverance. . . . He's walking along, because he's in charge of all the safety now to make sure all the entrances and everything are secure and if there's any problems underground then he can get that taken care of. He's walking along and all of sudden here comes this guy walking. They kind of nodded hello at each other. He turned around and the guy wasn't there and there was nowhere to go because it was inside the tunnel and everything is solid rock."

A few years previously my girlfriend, MC, called this man, hoping to interview him about the experience. She asked him if he had had an odd encounter underground.

"Yeah, but I'm not telling you about it!" he replied and hung up.

Brian, Renee, and other mine explorers come upon areas where odd graffiti is often found. Renee found a swastika that had been painted before the Nazi Party rose to power.

"It would just feel kind of eerie when you get back into some of those places," Renee said. "Another friend of ours went way back in an area in the mine that was actually still intact. It hadn't been high graded. All the stuff was still there. He said it just felt like they were still there. He felt like he was on a shift change."

She rarely hears clear words from the ghosts. "You can tell when they get excited. There's a group of them talking. Occasionally I make out a word or two. I can definitely hear them laughing. Sometimes I talk to them. 'Come on guys, leave me alone.' I think they're an echo of what they were most of the time, but every once in a while . . . they know we're here and they respect what we're doing. If we were doing something that was not respectful of them, what their focus and priorities and intentions are, then I think they might be a little more upset with us."

The sun had set and twilight shuddered on the lonely valley when I thanked Renee for her time and stories. I paused on the bridge over Gold Creek and stared at the swift current of black water. I felt a little creeped out, like I was being observed by something in the darkness. It didn't feel evil or annoyed, just watchful. Fenrir was curled up in the driver's seat when I got back. She lay her head in my lap as we drove through the thick darkness home.

THE TERRIBLE FATE

OF THE SS *CLARA NEVADA*

THROUGHOUT history many mariners have adhered to superstitions that landlubbers find unusual. One favorite was that no woman should be allowed on a boat, due to the fact she'd be too distracting. There was a loophole, though. Chicks could sail if they were naked—for the obvious reason that their smokin' hot bods would calm stormy seas. This belief dates back to when people bathed twice during their life and a fleeting glimpse of a feminine ankle was such a giddy experience that it inspired verses of poetry, bawdy songs, and an epidemic of venereal disease. Some archaic beliefs die hard. I remember one commercial fishing captain I worked for, a kind but tightly strung man, who threatened to throw me overboard when he caught me whistling.

"You'll summon a storm!" he yelled.

"I'm sorry," I said, peeling a banana.

"You brought a banana aboard! That's bad luck!" he squealed, swinging a salmon gaff at the fruit. "Throw it overboard and go wash your hands in bleach!"

"Do you mind if invite my friend Ginger aboard? She has some really good ideas for renaming your boat. How does *Drowned Good Luck* sound?" I asked.

He sobbed and danced around like an orangutan trying to do ballet. I learned a lot that season about what you can and can't do on a boat. For instance, gingers have no souls and have been the doom of many a fisherman. Bananas are the devil's fruit and have doomed many mariners. Certain words and phrases like "drown" and "good luck" must never be said on a boat and can lead to doom.

Most interestingly, I also learned I had the power of making people go bat-guano crazy. It was both sad and a relief when I loaded my captain—drooling and spouting gibberish about being a little teapot and begging me to not hit another whale during my wheel watch—on a plane bound for the Alaska Psychiatric Institute.

The greatest taboo by far, the superstition that makes even the most skeptical sailor shudder, is that you can't change the name of a boat without encouraging doom. There are certain circumstances, such as totally rebuilding a vessel, in which renaming is acceptable. It's still a good idea to light some firecrackers, drink a half rack of beer, and spray the bow with the blood of a sacrificial virgin of some sort before the newly christened boat's first voyage. Of all the horrible tragedies in Southeast Alaska's maritime history, the SS *Hassler*, renamed the *Clara Nevada* for its last voyage, lends the most credence to this great maritime superstition. On February 5, 1898, the *Clara Nevada* crashed into Eldred Rock, a tiny barren islet, marooned in Lynn Canal's savage expanse of ocean and mountains. All aboard were thought to have perished—the speculated count varied from 25 to 150, an indication of how wild and unregulated life was during the Klondike gold rush.

Steven C. Levi, an Anchorage writer, authored the book *The Clara Nevada; Gold, Greed, Murder and Alaska's Inside Passage*, which resurrected the story of the *Clara Nevada* from its watery grave. Levi has probably researched the wreck better than anyone. He estimates the best count for casualties at around fifty-seven. Quite a few people, Levi included, believe the wreck was no accident and that Eldred Rock is the site of Alaska's biggest mass murder since the United States purchased the territory in 1867.

Lynn Canal, stretching from just north of Juneau to Haines and Skagway, is one of the longest and deepest fjords in the world. It is the northern limit of the Inside Passage. When John Muir arrived in 1879, and for hundreds of years before, the Auk, Chilkat, and Chilkoot Tlingit clans lived, traded, and warred along its shores. They're still here today, but settled in towns. Elsewhere, along the coast, graves and villages are rapidly being swallowed into the hungry rain forest. Petroglyphs of seemingly tormented anthropomorphic beings, salmon, and swirls adorn moss-covered boulders in the shadowy woods. Wolves, bears, moose, mountains goats, and a host of other wildlife live in the surrounding rain forest. Mountains rise up to 7,000 feet in a couple of miles, and beyond their jagged summits lies one of the biggest non-polar ice caps in the world. During Captain George Vancouver's 1791–95 voyage of the Pacific Northwest, the captain renamed the waterway after King's Lynn, his birthplace in England. The name couldn't be less fitting.

During the Klondike gold rush, Lynn Canal was the last stretch of ocean most stampeders traveled before they commenced on a long, difficult, dangerous adventure overland. Pierre Berton, Canada's great academic yarner, wrote, "The Klondike stampede did not start slowly and build up to a climax, as did so many earlier gold rushes. It started instantly with the arrival of the *Excelsior* and *Portland*, reached a fever pitch at once, and remained at fever pitch until the following spring, when, with the coming of the Spanish-American War, the fever died as swiftly as it arose." Both the *Excelsior* and the *Portland* were carrying hairy, smelly, half-mad bush-rat prospectors laden with literally tons of gold. The two ships reached San Francisco and Seattle mid-July in 1897. News spread faster than the yeast infections the suddenly rich Yukon men gave to fancy whores. More than 100,000 men, and some women, dropped what they were doing and headed north. The word on the street was that gold nuggets were everywhere, even growing on the stunted trees of the Yukon. All you needed was a bucket, a shovel, and a way to get there.

Steven C. Levi wrote, "In the Klondike stampede of 1898, as in all other gold rushes, entrepreneurs learned quickly that there was more money to be had from the pockets of the stampeders than out of ground. The greatest scams were not in the sales of fry pans, trousers, flour or shovels; they were in transportation. Stampeders had to go north—a high demand; the number of ships was limited—a low supply. Thus, by that natural mechanism, the shipping industry was destined to make money—lots of money." Nearly anything that floated was advertised as a first-class steamer and used to transport prospectors. Overcrowded derelict ships went down left and right, but the yellow madness was so strong that prospectors ignored the dangers and inflated prices. The quickest and most popular route to the Klondike was to sail up the Inside Passage to its northern limit and then trek overland through the mountains to the Yukon River. Numerous other routes were attempted, some fraudulently advertised by shipping companies as being easier, such as the impassable route several thousand prospectors attempted over the Valdez Glacier. The "rich man's route" involved sailing across the Gulf of Alaska up the Bering Sea to the mouth of the Yukon River and then catching a steamer up to Dawson. Levi writes, "By March 1898, the *Review of Reviews* estimated that stampeders spent over $60 million in supplies and tickets, of which Seattle was credited with receiving $16 million. But by the end of the year, the total Klondike output was estimated at only $10 million. . . . Of the estimated 100,000 people who actually set out after gold, only 30,000 made it as far as Dawson. About 15,000 of those looked for gold, but only 1 out of every 3 prospectors actually found any. Of these, no more than 300 became wealthy." To those statistics, the Klondike Gold Rush National Historical Park in Seattle adds that only fifty prospectors retained their wealth for any length of time.

Before the gold rush, the SS *Hassler* was used primarily for surveying the coast and islands of the Pacific Northwest. It operated for twenty-five years before it was deemed no longer seaworthy. The McGuire brothers, remembered for their capitalistic zeal and lack of morals, purchased, refurbished, and renamed the vessel the *Clara Nevada*. The ship set sail from Seattle on January 26, 1898, loaded with, according to the National Oceanic and Atmospheric Administration, "165 passengers and about 40 crew members." The captain, C. H. Lewis, kept families in both Baltimore and San Francisco. According to Levi's research, Lewis's sailing resume was filled with one disaster and wild adventure after the next. At fifteen he went by sea to get in on the California gold rush of 1849. He smuggled weapons to the Confederacy during the Civil War. Later, numerous ships under his command wrecked, caught fire, and sunk. Most of these accidents seemed to be a result of ineptitude, but there was an ominous undertone to Lewis's life long before the *Clara Nevada*. He, by all accounts, was a man who let money guide his moral compass. It's indicative of the nature of the frontier that Lewis was able to keep captaining boats. When Lewis attempted to pull the *Clara Nevada* out of Seattle, he continued his run of mayhem and madness. Levi writes that passenger Charles Jones was quoted as saying, "I was afraid the *Clara Nevada* would be wrecked from the time she left Seattle until Skagway was reached. We smashed into the revenue cutter *Grant* when we were backing out of Yesler's Dock; we rammed into almost every wharf we tried to land; we blew out three (boiler) flues; we floundered around in rough waters until all passengers were scared almost to death; we witnessed intoxication among the officers and heard them cursing each other until it was sickening."

The *Clara Nevada* was illegally carrying a load of dynamite (reportedly a year's worth for the gigantic Treadwell Mine) that was to be delivered to Treadwell City on Douglas Island. Apparently, due to the constant fiascoes, bad weather, and delays, Captain Lewis decided to forgo the delivery. He sailed past Douglas Island, up the northern limit of Stephens Passage, and into the treacherous waters of Lynn Canal. The passengers were undoubtedly eager to be off the foundering craft. At Skagway they off-loaded their huge outfits and were greeted with the sprawling mayhem of humanity, strewn beneath formidable mountains and howling winds. From here they could choose to travel either the Chilkoot Trail from Dyea or the White Pass Trail from Skagway. Both trails were relatively short and ended at Lake Bennett, the headwaters of the Yukon River. However, the Canadian Mounted Police required each prospector to carry 2,000 pounds of supplies over the mountains before they could build some sort of craft to float the Yukon River to the goldfields. This requirement minimized the number of fatalities, particularly from starvation, in Canada. Alaska was a different story. The first year of the gold rush, Skagway, Dyea, and their respective trails were remembered as lawless free-for-alls. Some describe the boomtowns as hell on earth, where shooting, knifings, and robberies happened nearly every night.

In a winter storm, Lynn Canal is about the last place on earth any sane person would want to be. The winds were said to be blowing snow at upward of eighty miles per hour when the *Clara Nevada* departed Skagway southbound on the fifth of February. I'm familiar with the fjord, and can say under those conditions that the ocean would be a complete chaos of stacked fifteen-foot-or-higher waves. Modern day ferries, bigger and 100 times more seaworthy than the *Clara Nevada,* would have remained tied up in port. An unknown number of passengers, most probably horrified and seasick, were tossed about in the wintry darkness, listening to the roar of crashing waves and howling of the storm. It's no surprise the ship, already near its death, went down in those conditions under the command of a wild and seemingly inept captain. Men at the Comet Mine located at the base of Lion's Head Mountain, some twelve miles from Eldred Rock, reported seeing a giant fireball when the ship wrecked. It would seem to indicate the vessel rammed into the rocky islet and its illegal store of dynamite exploded. As insane as the last voyage of the *Clara Nevada* was, all this makes sense considering the history of the vessel and the captain. There were said to be no survivors, though a lifeboat was found washed up on the shore.

The *Clara Nevada,* as strange and haphazard as her short second lease on life had been, was written off as another byproduct of the epidemic of yellow madness that captivated the world and plunged the north into chaos. It was a clear accident motivated by greed. Yet, in the years after, rumors began to circulate. The first indication something more sinister might have happened was after numerous teams of divers failed to find the shipment of gold the vessel was said to be carrying. Levi claims the *Clara Nevada* was carrying $165,000 worth of gold (worth nearly $12 million in today's market) when it wrecked in less than thirty feet of water. It seems like it would be relatively easy to recover the gold. Unless someone else had already taken it. Numerous other odd inconsistencies appeared. For one, Captain Lewis and a few of the crew seem not to have been aboard when the ship went down. They would have had to somehow escape the explosion and row a lifeboat through fifteen-foot choppy waves to shore. From there, they would have had to travel through an extremely rugged wilderness covered in deep snow for dozens of miles, crossing rivers to get to Haines or Skagway. Neither is possible. Levi and many others believe Lewis and a few crew members set a small charge of dynamite next to the *Clara Nevada's* boilers in order to steal the vessel's shipment of gold. One theory is that a few miles beforehand, the criminals managed to escape in a lifeboat of some sort to Haines, where the water was more protected, on the west side of Lynn Canal. Somehow the ship continued on before exploding on Eldred Rock. It seems like a wild theory too, but in those crazy times just about anything was possible.

Despite the fact he was supposed to be dead, Captain C. H. Lewis began to show up in logs soon after the disaster. Levi writes, "It appeared that Lewis was able to survive a sinking, find passage back to Seattle, buy a steamboat for cash, cross the United States to Baltimore where he registered the steamer, return to the West Coast to outfit the ship, hire a crew and be back in business in a mere 116 days." This endeavor ended with his steamer lost and stranded on a sandbar long before reaching Dawson City and the Klondike goldfields. Levi says Lewis died from old age, taking the mystery of the *Clara Nevada* to his grave.

These days multitudes of boats, everything from behemoth cruise ships to kayaks, travel Lynn Canal every summer. Early one April, I set off alone up Lynn Canal in an old kayak. It was a misty, calm morning and the deep booming of sooty grouse echoed from rugged mountains rising into blue sky. I passed Vanderbilt Reef, where the *Princess Sophia* went down in 1918, taking all 350 or so aboard with her. Sea lions, land otters, and harbor seals eyed me curiously. In Berners Bay, a host of newly arrived species of waterfowl and seabirds—marbled murrelets, pigeon guillemots, Barrow's goldeneyes, long-tailed ducks, Pacific loons—many still in their white winter plumage, parted as my kayak slid past. Soon eulachon—followed by thousands of hungry seagulls, eagles, sea lions, humpback whales, seals, and other species converging to feast—would return to the river deltas to spawn. I turned the corner at Point St. Mary, and stared up the fjord at an expanse of blue and rugged mountains. Choppy seas and a large group of sea lions demanded my attention. I pulled hard to the right to keep from colliding with one as it bobbed contentedly inside a wave.

Near Point Sherman, a few buildings and a short road led to the Comet Mine and tailings pile along the ramparts of Lion's Head Mountain. Beaches disappeared into nearly vertical mountains jutting straight from the ocean. Glaciers clung to all but the most vertical summits. The coastline would remain nearly impenetrable, broken only by dozens of avalanche paths, until Skagway. That night I sat on the little bit of sandy beach, boiling water on my camp stove for a cup of tea and pasta. A pack of wolves had been here not long before, leaving behind lots of tracks and a few scats filled with bits of bones and mountain goat hair. The last time I was at this spot a friend had set me ashore and then went to anchor his skiff. He started yelling and waving his arms wildly after he saw a brown bear checking me out from the nearby alders. On the skiff ride home, as we were rocked and soaked by six-foot waves, I vowed to never again be so foolish as to venture into Lynn Canal in

November in a small craft. Presently, I finished my dinner and stared out at the calm seas. A pod of killer whales passed, just barely visible in the twilight.

In the morning, I bobbed in two-foot seas and stared at Eldred Rock Lighthouse glowing beneath the Chilkat Mountains. Eight years after the *Clara Nevada*, a lighthouse was built on Eldred Rock. In 1908, during an exceptionally violent March storm, the assistant lighthouse keeper reported that the *Clara Nevada* was dredged up onto shore and that corpses, or at least skeletons of the doomed, were strewn about. A short while later, during the same storm, monster waves washed the ship and its passengers back under the sea. Renee Hughes, the Sentinel Lighthouse keeper, stationed around thirty miles to the south in Lynn Canal, believes just about every lighthouse in Southeast Alaska has ghosts. She's not alone in believing the fjord is haunted—as I bobbed in the waves, feeling vulnerable and open to Lynn Canal, I knew there was life, death, and mystery in these waters beyond my understanding. The *Clara Nevada* and its terrible fate was one more piece in Southeast Alaska's eerie history. I paddled on, remembering not to whistle, toward the end of the Inside Passage.

6.

THE KING CON
OF THE KLONDIKE

IN July of 1898, Mary Smith and her eldest son boarded a train in St. Louis and headed west. Outside the coach window, images of forests and loggers, farms and cattle and lonesome communities sprouted from the earth rattled by. The bison, bears, and wolves were all but vanished. The Indians were decimated, beaten, and confined. Some of the other passengers talked of the last great adventure of the West, the Klondike gold rush, as the young woman closed her eyes and was unable to fall asleep.

Two thousand miles later, the Smiths arrived in Seattle, a city seemingly sprung to life overnight. Many men, recently returned from the Klondike, wandered the streets with hollow guts and wild eyes. They offered the diminutive woman sober smiles. Perhaps the young mother and her son reminded them of the families they'd left behind. Perhaps they were afraid to go home. What, after all, do you tell your wife and children after being gone for a year of adventure, toil, and madness with no riches to show for your sacrifice? The mountains, rivers, and people they'd met "on the trail" would soon exist only in memories and nightmares. For the lucky ones, the Klondike would haunt their days like a good sort of nostalgia as they worked in factories, slaughterhouses, or at desk jobs. Some just didn't happen to find any gold. Others had lost their money and outfits to the king con in Skagway, a man named Jeff Randall Smith, more commonly known as Soapy Smith, who happened to be Mary's husband.

Jeff and Mary met late in 1885 when she was thirteen or fourteen and working as a performer at Denver's Palace Theater. The story goes a man accosted Mary and was about to make off with her when Jeff knocked the barbarian out. He proceeded to sweep the girl away on a two-month romance before marrying her. There had to have been something special about Mary, because Jeff, an up-and-coming handsome hustler, could have had his pick of ladies. One picture of Mary from around the time they married shows a pretty, innocent-looking girl. Jeff kept Mary in St. Louis and visited her and their children frequently.

One of Jeff's most well-known swindles was the soap game. It was a sort of lottery involving a pile of bars of soap—a few had money under their wrappers—except no one ever won but Smith. The story goes that on one occasion he was arrested and a police officer gave him the nickname of "Soapy," which according to his great-grandson, he hated. Smith preyed upon mining boomtowns, running a large and intricate bunco gang. He and his men were hired out by politicians to help folks vote for the "right" candidate. One of his more creative scams was "the Petrified Man," a life-size figure made out of cement and plaster someone found in a Denver junkyard. Smith acquired the statue and promptly claimed he'd found the body of the missing link. He put it on display in Creede, Colorado, and charged a fee for a look. After supposedly making thousands, Smith leased the "the Petrified Man" to another entrepreneur for a national tour.

While not a killer, Jeff was no stranger to violence. Creede and Denver, where he spent the majority of his career, were full of men who solved disputes with pistols, knives, or anything else ready at hand. If a fight came, Smith rose to meet it, but he by far preferred to separate men from their money in a peaceful manner. By the late 1890s, civilization had just about ended opportunities in the West for men like Smith. He'd become so infamous in Colorado he was having difficulty operating his gang. What he needed was a new frontier and another gold rush to take advantage of. He got his wish when the SS *Portland* and SS *Excelsior* showed up in Seattle and San Francisco in the middle of July in 1897 with news of a gold strike. Smith quickly departed north to scout the best place to set up his operation. First he sailed across the Gulf of Alaska to St. Michael, once a Russian-American Company post and now a Yup'ik Eskimo village, on the Yukon-Kuskokwim River Delta. Not finding the lonely clutch of humanity to his liking, Smith sailed back to the Inside Passage and visited Dyea and Skagway.

Some people said Skagway in those days was "hell on earth." Pierre Berton, Canada's acclaimed academic storyteller, wrote in his book *Klondike Fever,* "The town of Skagway was conceived in lawlessness and nurtured in anarchy." The first stampeders, including a mysterious schoolteacher and Indian fighter named Frank Reid, bullied the Moore family, Skagway's first homesteaders, off "their land." Shootings were said to take place almost nightly. Stroller White, a treasured columnist of the north, was nearly hit by stray bullets one night while sleeping in his office. The most tragic and well-known murder happened January 31, 1898, at one of the dozens of drinking establishments. The accounts vary, but what is not disputed is that a drunk and disgruntled patron named Andrew McGrath was potentially robbed and then thrown out of a bar. He sought the assistance of a young marshal named James Marks Rowan, who was busy searching for a doctor for his wife as she was about to give birth to their first child. McGrath was so persuasive that Rowan followed him into the bar to settle the dispute. The bartender, thinking the two men were coming to shoot the place up, opened fire, killing McGrath outright and mortally wounding Rowan. Shortly before his child was born, Rowan died. Some believe his angry ghost haunts the town to this day.

Legend has it that Jeff Smith jumped in and prevented the

bartender from being lynched and then set up a charity account for the young widow and her child. Berton wrote, "Slowly and very quietly, almost without realizing it, the community became aware of a man named Jefferson Randall Smith, the same Soapy Smith who had announced in Seattle that he would be the boss of Skagway. By midwinter he had made good his boast. Over its citizens and transients he held the power of life and death. Before he was through, he had his own army—drilled, disciplined, and armed—his own spy system, and his own secret police. He cowed the militia and bought out the civil law. Merchants, businessmen, and journalists were in his pocket, and his sway extended along both Dyea and Skagway trails to the very summit of the passes, where the Northwest Mounted Police installed Maxim guns to keep him at bay."

Smith found optimal grounds in the makeshift chaos for his operations. His methods of thievery and swindles were nearly endless. They included the soap game, three-card monte, the shell game, fake packing companies, a fake telegraph company, and a landing committee that would help "organize" freight for stampeders when they disembarked from a steamer onto the expansive tide flats of the Skagway and Dyea Rivers. His gang was known to commit good old-fashioned muggings, but for the most part Smith was more creative. One account says he posed as a coroner on the Chilkoot Trail when spring avalanches killed dozens so he could unburden corpses of anything valuable. There was an endless procession of new and naive men passing through the town on their way to hump 2,000 pounds over the White Pass Trail to Lake Bennett. Smith made a point of preying on transients and leaving residents alone. By most accounts he was quite popular and likely well on his way to taking up "honest" work like politics after the gold rush.

Many people tell stories of Smith's generosity to people and animals in need. He has even been dubbed a Robin Hood several times. Supposedly he raised money to build Skagway's first church, a story the minister did his best to discredit. When prospectors abandoned multitudes of dogs in Skagway after finding them no help lugging their outfits over the trail, Smith created a pet adoption agency. He was said to have provided for widows who lost their husbands to the perils of the Chilkoot and White Pass Trails. He'd raise money for unlucky men who'd lost their outfits, quite frequently because of his gang, so they could book passage home. When the Spanish-American War broke out, Smith created and drilled a Skagway company. It was probably largely for show, but it makes clear his civic savvy and knowledge of public relations. By May 28, 1898, when construction began on the White Pass Railroad, Smith ought to have realized his grasp on Skagway would soon end. Civilization had caught up with him again. Most men would have garnered their winnings and headed out. But Smith was no normal man. A gambler who perhaps fell prey to his own legend, he was well on his way to making the biggest bluff of his life.

Mary Smith booked tickets on a steamer up the Inside Passage bound for Skagway. For the first time ever, mother and son looked out on the undulating expanse of the Pacific Ocean. They sailed north, staring up at the rain forest mountains and studying their shades of gray. They steamed past Vancouver Island and logging camps at the base of fir- and cedar-covered hills and mountains. The occasional pod of whales may have broken the water's surface, although commercial whaling was at its peak and had greatly depleted populations. They passed Native villages and camps abandoned because of disease, missionary efforts, and economic opportunities. At least one passenger, according to her great-grandson Jeff Smith, who wrote the biography *Alias Soapy Smith*, fell in love with her during the passage. In ensuing months, the man, a lonely prospector out of Dawson, wrote eleven times, begging her to move north to be with him.

The forest grew wilder and the mountains grew taller. They stopped in Wrangell at the mouth of the great Stikine River. Tlingit women sold berries, baskets, and trinkets from shore. Eagles circled overhead and ravens watched with sideways glances from the branches of spruce and hemlock trees. Some of her husband's gang were said to have operated in the rough little community; some rumors even have it that Smith would flee to hide out in Wrangell when things got too hot in Skagway.

They sailed north through Sumner Strait, Frederick Sound, and Stephens Passage to the large-scale mining ports of Juneau, Douglas, and Treadwell. The sound of stamp mills crushing ore echoed back and forth across Gastineau Channel as miners of all ethnicities labored in the bowels of the earth. The boat pulled around the southern tip of Douglas Island and chugged north up the great fjord of Lynn Canal. By now many of the passengers probably knew who Mary was, and they likely watched her with a mixture of fascination, disgust, and pity. It wasn't easy being married to a legendary, charismatic criminal. Newspapers had reported Jeff dead numerous times in the past decade. He'd told Mary that unless she saw his corpse, she shouldn't believe the stories. How Smith stayed alive as long as he did showed a real talent for survival.

By June of 1898, Skagway was an increasingly contentious community. Smith, while in deep with many Skagway business owners, was well on his way to a showdown with other powerful men and companies that wanted to rule the port. According to Pierre Berton, "Half the people of Skagway saw Smith as the devil incarnate. Half saw him as a good fellow and public-spirited townsman trying to bring order out of chaos. . . . By April (1898), Smith's organization numbered somewhere between two and three hundred confidence men, harlots and pimps, thugs and cardsharps. . . . " In contrast, Catherine Holder Spude, author of *"That Fiend in Hell": Soapy Smith in Legend,* believes Smith's power was grossly overestimated. Either way, big forces were at work in Skagway, and Smith would soon meet with a power some might argue was equally corrupt, but which operated in a manner better accepted by society.

John Douglas Stewart was a prospector with a poke full of gold who'd recently traveled from the Klondike goldfields to Skagway, arriving July 8. He was promptly waylaid by members of Smith's gang. Stroller White, who was on scene, reported: "There are conflicting stories as to how the robbery was committed, the accepted version being that Stewart desired to sell his gold, and that one Bowers, a well-known member of Smith's gang, represented to Stewart that he was here for the purpose of buying gold for some big assaying company below. The unsuspecting stranger accompanied Bowers to a point in the rear of Smith's place on Holly Avenue, and near the Mondamin Hotel, where it is alleged, two of Bowers' pals were in waiting, where the three men overpowered Stewart, wrested the sack of gold, containing $2670, from his hands, and disappeared from sight around adjoining buildings, leaving the returned Klondiker as poor as when he started for the land of gold and hardships nearly a year before."

Skagway's businessmen were horrified to hear of such a brash mugging of a returning prospector. After all, if other men, weighed down with gold, feared to pass through Skagway and chose to steam down to St. Michael, the town would greatly suffer. An ultimatum, stating the gold be returned and that all bunco men get out of town or else, was delivered to Smith. He "partially" promised to do so by four o'clock that same evening. By late afternoon, townspeople saw Smith drinking heavily and yelling—two things he apparently rarely did. Business owners called a meeting of several hundred vigilantes to take place at the end of the Juneau Wharf to decide what to do about Smith and his gang. Four men, including Frank Reid and Jesse Murphy, were chosen to guard the dock and prevent any of Smith's gang from infiltrating the meeting.

The last moments of Smith's life were so unlike the rest of his time alive that it leaves me wondering. In some way, since the frontier was closing and the gold rush was over, did he feel like he had nowhere to go? Probably not, but it's a pretty thought. People would write dozens of books and even more articles about him. He's inseparable from the Klondike—an honor I find a little amusing, since he never ventured near the goldfields or moved an ounce of dirt with a pick, shovel, or pan. Skagway was where he'd made a legacy, and it's where he'd die.

Smith finished his drink and stalked toward the Juneau Wharf, armed with a rifle and pistol. He apparently knew and strongly disliked

Frank Reid, so he approached him and the two squared off just feet apart.

Not that much is known about Reid. Jeff Smith, the author and great-grandson of the outlaw Smith, had few kind things to say about him. The man by all accounts was rough and well-known as an Indian fighter, schoolteacher, and surveyor. It seems quite probable he was more interested in capitalistic gain than morality when he played a part in pushing Skagway's first white homesteaders off their land. Smith's great-grandson also wrote about him murdering a neighbor in a dispute from which the courts allowed him to walk free. Some believe Reid may even have worked for Smith at one time, but they rubbed each other the wrong way.

Most accounts say that Smith attempted to strike Reid with the barrel of his rifle. Reid grabbed hold of the rifle, drew his pistol, and aimed it at Smith.

"My God, don't shoot!" Smith supposedly yelled, and both shot. Smith fell dead and Reid lay mortally wounded by a shot through his groin. That's how most stories go.

There's another account. Jesse Murphy—a basically unknown Irish railroad worker—grabbed or wrestled away Smith's rifle after Reid shot Smith in the leg. He turned the rifle on the wounded outlaw. Smith's great-grandson believes this is when Soapy yelled, "My God, don't shoot!" Murphy, perhaps jacked up from the gun battle or wanting to make sure Smith's reign was ended, shot the fallen man through the chest, killing him instantly. He then turned the rifle on some of Smith's gang, who'd been trailing their leader. They scattered to hide in the woods.

Reid died nearly two weeks later and was immortalized with a giant, elaborate grave marker that bears the inscription, "He gave his life for the town of Skagway." Smith was buried at the edge of the graveyard and given a decrepit marker with only his name, age, and the date of his death. In the north's, and the nation's, initial narrative of the gunfight, Reid died the hero of civilization and Smith died the devil at the edge of the wilderness. Soon it would turn into a legend and a gimmick for Skagway shops and tours selling Klondike mythology to visitors.

Mary and her son, according to her great-grandson Jeff Smith, arrived in Skagway "the morning of August 3, 1898." In time the community went from being openly hostile to friendly. She visited her husband's grave, and was convinced of his passing. Smith supposedly had virtually nothing in his estate—no valuables or money. On August 23, Mary and her son sailed back toward home carrying with them little more than their memories.

7.

The Ghosts of
Skagway

I N April of 2009, after spending a month and a half wandering the eastern Brooks Range in the Arctic, I was returning home to Juneau. The ferry was full when I showed up to Skagway and the next sailing south was a few days from departing. To kill time, I hiked a mountain up into the clouds and followed the tracks of a brown bear who'd recently emerged from its winter sleep through wet snow. A heavy musk emanated from the tracks, but perhaps it was me—I'd only had one cold shower in almost two months. The tracks were just a couple of hours old. To the south, shrouded in somber clouds, stretched Lynn Canal and the Coast and Chilkat Mountain Ranges. Below were two valleys, one leading from Dyea to the Chilkoot Pass and the other leading from Skagway to the White Pass. At the ocean's edge was the small sprawl of Skagway, surrounded on all sides by wilderness. The docks were empty and the town seemed asleep. It was hard to imagine that in a month and a half, thousands of tourists would flood the tiny town each day. Many would off-load where Soapy Smith, Alaska's most legendary outlaw, was shot and killed. It would sound like one more hokey story from the canon of the American West, soon to be forgotten in a capitalistic buzz and swirl oddly reminiscent of Bangkok, New Orleans, and Las Vegas.

Few events in Alaska's history better embody frontier mythology than the Klondike gold rush. Close to 100,000 men and women flooded the wild north in just a few years. Greed, adventure, and madness—nearly 120 years later, the romanticism of their herculean efforts still radiates. It shines the brightest at the northern limit of the Inside Passage, in the port of Skagway.

Some say the gold rush town is the most haunted community in Southeast Alaska, and that if you visit the Red Onion Saloon, Golden North Hotel, or other buildings, you stand a decent chance of encountering a ghost. People hiking the Chilkoot Trail, the iconic route on which more than 30,000 stampeders hauled 2,000-pound outfits to the headwaters of the Yukon River, have reported ghosts. The White Pass Trail saw an equal amount of traffic, but a highway has replaced the trail. Skagway, along with its sister community, Dyea, now a ghost town, sprang to messy life overnight with the arrival of the first stampeders in 1897. Before that, both town sites were used as camps and trade routes by the Chilkat and Chilkoot Tlingits. In its first few years as a permanent community, the population fluctuated wildly, sometimes up into the tens of thousands. Prostitutes, bunco men, and equally immoral and predatory businessmen followed the stampeders north. John Muir famously described Skagway in 1897 as "a nest of ants taken into a strange country and stirred up by a stick."

"Skagway is very haunted," Cori Giacomazzi, curator of the museum at the Red Onion Saloon, told me. The Red Onion was one of many dance halls and brothels that sprang up in 1897. Today it's the best bar and pizza joint in town; during the summer, tour guides dressed as madams offer walking tours of the town and the brothel, many of which have a ghostly theme. The brothel has ten rooms, popularly known as cribs, where prostitutes once plied their trade. Cori clammed up a little when I made the mistake of mentioning I was skeptical, a rookie error when you're interviewing someone about supernatural and paranormal experiences. Instead of shutting me down, she warned that the Red Onion's most active ghost, whom she called Lydia, has a penchant for messing with skeptics. Cori had her first experience with the ghost more than a decade ago. She was in the brothel rearranging artifacts with her mentor, Billy Clem, when she suddenly felt a presence behind her. It wasn't threatening, but Cori did admit she was creeped out.

"Do you see Lydia?" Billy asked. More often than not, Cori feels rather than sees her.

My girlfriend, MC, interviewed some of the Red Onion staff in 2013 for an article for the *Capital City Weekly*. She wrote that "Operations Manager Liz Lavoie said Lydia is often seen in a corner of what's known as the 'wallpaper room,' where a nickel-plated dress found in a trunk more than 30 years ago hangs on display. Some hypothesize that she may have hung herself there, though Lavoie said that's nothing she could verify. Some also hypothesize that she may have hung herself after contracting syphilis and losing her ability to work. One woman who used to work at the Red Onion saw Lydia once, Lavoie said, and said she had a branding on her face. Sex workers were sometimes branded as diseased so that they couldn't keep working, Lavoie said. She added, however, that what may have happened to Lydia is all guesswork."

"Lydia is a very needy ghost," Cori told me.

Her history is pieced together largely by mediums. Cori heard she came to Skagway during the gold rush with a man and lived a respectable life for a while. The man may have abandoned her or died on the trail. Regardless, Cori said, "Women could only make $3 a day and the cost of living was $6 a day."

Feeling trapped, Lydia went to work as a prostitute. Cori claims Lydia isn't malevolent, although she doesn't like most men. She can't stand being ignored and definitely does not appreciate skeptics. Once, a cynical madam was leading a tour of the brothel when—perhaps she made a disparaging remark—a metal bed frame rose into the air and smacked against the wall three times. That same day garters went flying when girls were changing in the dressing room. Another madam was tapped on her shoulder by an unseen presence. Lydia, according to Cori, is quirky. Apparently, unless you acknowledge her aloud, you can't get into the safe. If you play hip-hop she'll get pissed, but hard rock is okay and cleaners have to sing in certain parts of the hotel or she'll make the vacuum cleaner explode.

MC interviewed Steve Bagwell, who worked as a security and maintenance man at the Red Onion for several years. He believed he may have crossed paths with a ghost there in June of 2013. He told MC, "I've never seen anything like that in my life. I was here all alone real early in the morning, and a woman—I was at the top of the stairs and down at the bottom of the stairs a woman crossed the room going really fast. It wasn't a normal walk. It was really fast."

"About 15 minutes later," MC wrote, "the same thing happened in the upstairs room where he was working. A woman crossed the room, moving faster than a person would walk.

"'That time I followed, and it was a dead end where I seen the woman go, and no one was there. And that's the only thing that's happened to me. Nothing was threatening or aggressive or nothing, but it gave me the willies,' he said. He said he couldn't see her face. She was wearing a dress and a shawl, she was slim and small, and he got the impression she was a woman on the younger side of middle-aged. She also looked solid, not transparent. That's the only time he's experienced anything like that, he said—there are lots of 'weird noises' in the building, but most of them could be blamed on the wind and the building's age."

When I asked Cori if there were other spirits active in the Red Onion, she became quiet.

"There's one more, but I don't like talking about him," she said after a long silence. "He's an asshole."

Cori said the negative encounters people have reported are because of this ghost. She won't speak of him when she's in the Red Onion—he scares her, and, unlike Lydia, doesn't want to be acknowledged. Cori pieced together that he was a bouncer and an abuser of women, and was knifed to death in the brothel. He frequents the dressing room when women are changing into their madam outfits. Once, Cori smelled horrible body odor in the center of the room. A friend came in and asked her about the stink. Slowly, the odor moved to a corner of the room. Cori was most disturbed recalling a young cook, an Alaska Native from Anchorage, who became plagued with nightmares in which the bouncer revealed the abuse he'd done to women in the Red Onion. The young man saw himself being murdered as the man had been. MC reported, "Not all experiences are positive or neutral: recently, a cook quit the Red Onion and left Skagway, because, according to a text he sent, he was being 'f-ed with on another level,' by a ghost, said Lavoie. Sometimes, men—never women—that work at the Red Onion have had 'more aggressive' encounters, she said, feeling, for example, a shove when walking down a staircase. Nothing aggressive had happened for quite a while until this cook began working there. 'He was feeling pretty tormented,' Lavoie said. 'He felt like it followed him home and took a more nightmarish sort of quality.'"

My friend Johanna Evans, a woman I grew up with and believe to be quite credible, was skeptical when she began working as a "madam" for the Red Onion. Now, she definitely believes there's something very odd going on there. She told me the negative ghost's name is Joe and that he is mean, stinky, and creepy.

"I think it's fascinating, but I haven't had a whole lot of experiences. I don't think I'm very susceptible," she said. A couple times Johanna has gotten weird feelings while giving tours but, afraid of eliciting a negative reaction from a ghost, she kept it to herself. Often things would move around in the brothel, or lights would turn off and on, but she was never sure whether or not it was other employees doing it. Her most disturbing scenario occurred during a short brothel tour, a fifteen-minute show-and-tell that didn't address the Red Onion's haunted history. She finished and let the tourists out the back door and down the stairs to the street. One woman, apparently intoxicated, hung back in the room with her.

"The woman has to let you know that the man doesn't own her," she told Johanna casually, before exiting down the stairs.

A minute stroll from the Red Onion Saloon is the Golden North Hotel and the dwelling place of Mary, Southeast Alaska's most famous ghost. Dennis and Nancy Corrington own the building. Dennis is the sort of guy you can't help but like. He ran traplines, owned a trading post in Nome, and mushed the Iditarod before moving to Skagway in the late 1970s. There he became quite successful in real estate and tourism, though, like a typical Alaskan, he's most proud of his contribution to the world of beer.

"I created spruce tip ale, though I stole the idea from Captain Cook," Dennis admitted. James Cook, one of the greatest explorers of all time, infused his crew's whiskey with spruce tips, which bud a light shade of green early each spring. The captain guessed correctly that the tips contain vitamin C and would stave off scurvy.

The Golden North was built during the madness and mayhem of the Klondike gold rush, and Mary's ghost is said to watch over the building. The legend goes that Mary's lover, perhaps fiancé, was one of the tens of thousands of men and women who toiled over either the Chilkoot or White Pass. He likely hacked a boat out of the forest near Lake Lindeman or Lake Bennett during the winter, and when spring came, he bobbed and floated down the mighty Yukon River. His mind was on gold, but the lonely expanse of taiga coming to life that spring must have warmed his weary spirit. Deep in the Yukon, along the banks of some unknown stream near Dawson City, he hit pay dirt. Suddenly a rich man, he sent a telegraph to Mary, summoning her from the Lower 48 to Skagway to await his return. Perhaps he was dreaming of the first-class suite they'd share on a steamer bound for Seattle. In the big city, they'd indulge in a few celebrations before buying a farm or some sort of business in a land less brutal than the north. Elated at the prospect of the new life before her, Mary came north. The jagged mountains, the near constant howling wind, and the lawless squalor of men and women possessed by greed and excitement must have been a lot to take in. She booked an extended stay at the Golden North Hotel in room twenty-three and waited.

The now rich man missed the woman he loved; he ached fiercely. Perhaps shortly before the river froze, he bought passage on a steamer chugging up the river to Whitehorse. The birch, poplars, and aspens blazed gold on the ancient hills and mountains. Snow was slowly creeping down from the summits. The air had a cold bite and smelled of fermenting highbush cranberries. There's no more beautiful time in that country than right before winter, but he was nervous to be carrying so much gold. He knew the insanity it inspired. The trip overland was harder—how he transferred his outfit can only be guessed—but there's a good chance it was on his back. He struggled over trails edged with the carcasses of pack animals and the rubbish of broken men's dreams. Forests had been massacred by saw and ax. Slate gray clouds swirled over the jagged mountains and giant glaciers of the Coast Mountain Range.

Mary suffered impatience, doubt, and the attention of lonely men as days grew shorter and the ocean crashed relentlessly with the wind and tides. Fall turned to winter. She paced her room, fearing the worst. There were stories of Soapy Smith and his gang of hoodlums. There were other fiends at work in town and along the trails, as well. She'd heard, perhaps even seen, shootings and knifings. There was no end to stories of men lost to suicide, murder, avalanches, drowning, exhaustion, and even heartbreak on the trail. Where her man met his end is unknown, but lore says he was robbed and murdered. His bloodied corpse was swallowed amidst the wreckage of the last great gold rush. After being told the news, Mary stopped eating, withered away, and died alone in her room.

At least, that's more or less how the story goes. Many folks say the tale and reports of ghosts are far from credible, but Dennis is a believer. There were many stories about Mary before Dennis and Nancy purchased the hotel. The evening Dennis closed on buying the hotel, he walked into the Golden North's bar to celebrate. He poured a scotch and a glass of beer; he hadn't had more than a couple sips before a strong perfume hit him.

"Hey, Mary. I'm Dennis Corrington. My wife, Nancy, and I are the new hotel owners," he said, feeling a little foolish. He proceeded to tell the seemingly empty room that he and his wife would respect any ghosts and that they were welcome to stay in the hotel. He left the bar to grab his suitcase, which was in a hotel room—he'd flown into town that day. Someone or something had opened it, taken out his clothes, and stacked them, nicely folded, on the bed. Unnerved, Dennis quickly repacked his suitcase and was hit again with a strong dose of perfume. He ran back to the hotel where he was staying to call his wife and tell her about the experience.

"I felt like I was being welcomed by Mary," Dennis said. Many folks, ghost hunters and skeptics alike, have had odd experiences since. Some guests have woken and reported they felt like they were being choked. (Common lore has it that Mary died from pneumonia.) During one remodel, while Nancy was climbing the stairs, a bucket spontaneously burst into flames. Another time Nancy purchased a dozen large Victorian pictures to decorate the walls and different rooms. There were thirteen inside the crate, even though the invoice said a dozen. The thirteenth picture shows a handsome woman, and the colors completely match the wallpaper and flooring of room twenty-three.

Recently, Dennis was having lunch with a carver whose art he purchases to sell at his galleries. A quiet man Dennis greatly respects, the two have been friends for thirty years. After eating they were walking down Broadway Street when the man stopped outside the Golden North Hotel. Dennis had a business meeting scheduled a few minutes later.

"Whoa," the man said. "There's a lot going on in that building!"

Dennis was surprised; his friend seemed to know little of the hotel's haunted history. The hotel had been closed down for a decade, but Dennis had a key in his pocket. Sensing something very interesting was about to happen, he led his friend into the dusty lobby. First, Dennis took him to rooms that didn't have reputations for paranormal activity. The man—Dennis had no idea he was "spiritual" but now refers to him as a medium—walked into a room and then backed out with his hands up.

He called his wife and told her she needed to come to the hotel, that the meeting would go fine without her. The couple followed their friend as he wandered the second floor. He entered Mary's room, began rocking, and went into a trance for twenty or twenty-five minutes. When he came back, he told Dennis and Nancy that the spirit of a woman was there. He described her clothing and said she was waiting as winter came for her lover, who had been murdered somewhere on the trail. She died, he said, shortly after being told the horrible news. The Corringtons followed the man as he explored the rest of the hotel. He went back into room twenty-three and entered a rocking trance. All of a sudden he smacked himself on the chest and then gripped his hands over his ribs. He claimed there were three spirits on the second level and there was a very angry and desperate man in the room with them. He'd been shot and killed while his wife had been giving birth to their son, which seems to refer to the slaying of Marshal James Rowan. I reached out to the medium, but he declined to be interviewed.

The Golden North Hotel has been shut down for more than ten years now, though Dennis is considering opening it back up for ghost tours. These days the bottom floor is rented out to tourist shops. When I asked about whether I could spread my sleeping bag out in room twenty-three and spend the night, this is what he told me:

"Probably not. The plumbing's been shut down. What are you going to do, shit out on the street?"

Writing about the Golden North and Red Onion inspired a sort of deja vu that took me back to an eerie encounter I had years ago while hitchhiking in Maine. In August of 2001, I bought a cheap mountain bike and a Rand McNally map of Canada. Two days later, I left Skagway and began pedaling east. I believed somewhere on the journey I'd be struck by an epiphany that would make life make sense. Soul-searching entries in my journal were gradually replaced with towns' names, distances traveled, weather patterns, and the occasional interaction I had with another person or wild animal. More than two months later, on the eastern edge of the continent near Halifax, I the Atlantic Ocean for the first time and was filled with a powerful emptiness.

My bicycle was broken when I crossed the border into Maine at the small town of Calais. There I spent sixty to seventy hours a week working with single moms at Dunkin' Donuts and an Irving gas station. Most of the town's men had vanished to prison, drugs, Florida, or death. I heard the women grumbling. Collapse of the timber industry, damn greenies, try wiping your ass with a spotted owl. I had no idea how to talk to them so I listened as they complained, joked, and gabbed. At both jobs, wages were six dollars an hour with no hope of a raise. Sometimes a woman would show up with a black eye. Occasionally, one would throw doughnut dough at me or gently tease me. One night at the Irving, I was working with a young mom who broke down.

"I'm better than this," she said, wiping tears away. "Would you leave with me tonight? We could grab a half rack of Michelob Light, go to Florida, and never look back."

Late at night, I walked back to my apartment and swept up the snow that had blown through the broken window during the day. I'd dress warmly, crawl into my sleeping bag, and begin reading Sartre, Camus, Kierkegaard, Dostoyevsky, or Heidegger—all existentialists. There was a frantic desperation to my reading, as if my life was a game show and I was running out of time to answer the million-dollar question. A lot of nights, through the apartment's thin walls, I heard a man yelling and a woman and little boy sobbing. In time I grew to want to kill the man. I thought about writing him a note telling him some bullshit like how fragile and sacred life is. I'm pretty sure I saw the woman once when I was behind the register at the Irving. She had prematurely graying hair and empty eyes. It was weird she didn't know I'd listened to her crying many sleepless nights. I wanted to apologize for all I didn't do but, instead, I only charged her for half the items she placed on the counter.

A month into my time in Calais, two teenage girls appeared. They were dirty and overweight, but that didn't keep a number of men from stopping at the corner where they spent hours in the cold waiting. They often came into the Irving and disappeared into the bathroom together for a half hour or more. A couple nights they followed me through the swirling snow to my apartment. One touched me on the shoulder and asked a question I didn't understand. I stuttered and they burst out giggling, then walked into a shoddy building echoing with the laughter of drunken men. This was not the ending to the "amazing" journey I wanted. There had been no epiphany, only a loneliness and malaise that grew with each passing day. My longing for the simplicity of my tent, open places, and solitude became so great it felt like a knot in my gut.

On Thanksgiving Day, I filled my backpack with my possessions and waited on the side of the highway with my thumb up. I vowed never to read existential works again. I felt incredibly free. My only regret was that I had done nothing for the woman and small boy, but I thought little of them. The unknown that lay between Maine and Alaska took my thoughts away from Calais. Every driver that picked me up that day shared intimate details of their lives. The almost-dead old man, alone with his demons. The Vietnam War veteran who teared up as he spoke about losing his son. The blue collar worker addicted to Diet Coke. A friendly gay man who offered to buy me dinner. I was let off south of Bangor, standing in the snow and watching the last of the sun waste away behind a birch forest. Minutes turned to an hour; the occasional car passed. In the darkness, a beat-up Honda Civic drove slowly past before pulling off a couple hundred yards away. After many minutes, it returned. A young, pretty, skeletally thin and pale woman invited me in. The moon shone across the snowy forest. She spoke excitedly. I should have realized something was wrong when she casually said she knew me from before, and then softly whispered she was my mother. I was nineteen and had virtually no experience with the opposite sex; for all I knew this was normal.

"Tell me of your life," she said. I couldn't remember the last time anyone wanted to know anything about me. Awkwardly, I told her the truth. I was incredibly privileged. My life was great. She smiled and began to laugh almost hysterically and then abruptly stopped.

"You've done so much," she said. "If I were able to live again, I'd like to do a lot of what you've done."

She murmured something about being dead and I felt an acute revulsion come over me. I didn't ask and she didn't say any more on the subject. Otherwise, the conversation during the rest of the drive seemed pretty normal, even pleasant. I started getting a little worried after she'd driven me hours past where she said she lived.

"I have to let you go here," she said, slamming on the brakes. I stepped out, bent over, and reached into the backseat to grab my backpack. I looked over to say good-bye but she wasn't there. The door was wide open. She was standing a few feet behind me, staring at me with an agonized look.

"You okay?" I asked. She stepped forward and hugged me hard. Not sure where to put my hands, I awkwardly placed them on her back, feeling the sharp juts of her spine and ribs. I thanked her for the ride, she pulled a U-turn, and I watched her brake lights disappear into the darkness. I walked down the road looking for a suitable place to pitch my tent for the night until the light from a hot pink church billboard lit up the woods and road. It read: "Jesus We Just Want To Thank You For Being So Good." I found a place beneath a giant oak tree near the church to sleep. The wind shifted ominously through naked branches as I stared up at the expanse of stars. I thought of the millions of years of death beneath me, the company of the people that day, how transitory it all is, and how that's okay, because trying to hold on only leaves you clinging to ghosts.

Weeks later, I made it to Bellingham, Washington, boarded an Alaska Marine Highway ferry, and began motoring up the Inside Passage toward home.

The ghosts of the Red Onion, the Golden North, and the women of Maine all smell of the same sort of abandonment—one that I feel powerless to do anything about. But that fall, heading home, and many times since, I've stared out at the night, and it's haunted me.

8.

THE KÓOSHDAA KÁA
CHRONICLES

DECADES ago, near Tenakee Springs, on Chichagof Island, my dad was sneaking through the rain forest's dark maze looking for Sitka black-tailed deer. He was no greenhorn to the woods of Southeast Alaska. He brought home deer, mountain goats, and bears he hunted for our food. My brothers and I combed their fur with our fingers, smelled their rich wild smell, and grew up on the sustenance of their tasty flesh and the stories they inspired. This hunt was different, though. Even now, he's still not sure what happened. He'd been quietly moving through the crepuscular forest, careful to avoid brush and stepping on branches or into sinkholes, watching for a flicker of an ear or the shape of an animal in the gloom, when a strange feeling overcame him.

"I remember seeing a deer walking through the mist and then, for some reason, sitting down at the base of a tree," he said. After an indefinite amount of time he woke up groggy, wandering deeper into the woods, clutching his rifle. He wasn't wearing his backpack, which contained all his hunting and survival gear. For hours he searched for his pack, becoming increasingly ill at ease, until darkness forced him from the woods. He's still not sure what was wrong with him or those woods that day. Many Southeast Alaskans would likely wonder if he'd had a run-in with the Kóoshdaa Káa, our region's boogeyman.

One of my earlier memories of hearing of the Kóoshdaa Káa comes with a morbid weight. I was twelve and at a friend's house. His dad had recently returned from a hunt on Chichagof Island and was frying venison backstrap for dinner.

"Dad says Chichagof is called Kóoshdaa Káa island," my friend said, and then looked up. "Why do they call it Kóoshdaa Káa island?"

"We don't talk about that," his dad said sharply, putting an end to the conversation. Later, my friend and I slipped out into the night to throw snowballs at cars. While hiding behind a sodden rotting log, we took turns embellishing the little we'd heard about the Kóoshdaa Káa. Neither of us were exactly sure what one was, but we knew it was some sort of shape-shifting monster, that it looked like a cross between a land otter and human, and that it captured and tortured people lost at sea or in the woods. Less than a year later, when my friend's dad vanished with three others when his boat went down in the frigid waters south of Juneau, we no longer talked about the Kóoshdaa Káa. For a year or so, we searched for images of Jesus and angels in the clouds.

Two decades had passed since. I looked out my window as the Taku Winds howled up Gastineau Channel, past the lights of a boat harbor and out onto the white froth of the ocean. I sipped cheap whiskey, sifted through notes, and then pushed the papers and journals aside. I had an impending deadline for a book and I was still barely scratching the surface of what I was trying to write about. I couldn't sleep, and I obsessed over stories of ghosts, monsters, and tragedies. Was this mental illness? The night before, while I was working at the mental health unit of Juneau's hospital, a patient, violent and out of his mind with fear, began screaming about the Kóoshdaa Káa. There wasn't much I could do other than try to assure him he was safe, that nothing could take him while I sat with him in his room. He took a break from yelling, stared at me wildly, and then spoke with a startling clarity.

"I'm not so sure of that."

I tried to make some sense of these cryptic memories but my attention was drawn back to the churning black ocean. Why had I taken on this project?

Three months earlier, in mid-August of 2015, my girlfriend, MC, was standing in as the editor of the *Capital City Weekly* newspaper. She had no features for the week's issue and asked me to write something. I gave her a story about strange legends surrounding Thomas Bay, near Petersburg, that recounted a number of prospectors encountering madness and fiendish creatures at the beginning of the twentieth century. Though it's never explicitly stated, most Southeast Alaskans believe the story is about the Kóoshdaa Káa. Many also believe it's nothing more than alcohol-inspired storytelling. A few days after my article went to print, local resident Carlton Smith reached out to me. Like me, and many born and raised in Southeast Alaska, Carlton had grown up both frightened and intrigued by the stories. We met for coffee a few days later. Smith is an Eagle who belongs to the Tall-fin Killer Whale House (Keet Gooshi Hit) of Klukwan. His Tlingit name is Sha na k'u wa, which in English means "in the image of the ancient people."

"I googled 'kushtaka' and the first thing that came up was Charlie Sheen," Carlton said, laughing. The popular, or colonized, spelling of Kóoshdaa Káa is Kushtaka. There are other variations as well, such as Kucda-qua, Kooshdakhaa, Koushta ka, and more. Names in English include Land Otter Men (land otters are different from sea otters, which many not familiar with the animals tend to think of first) and Slim Men.

Carlton and I swapped stories. He told of strange experiences and feeling like he was being watched by something malevolent at his cabin at Chilkat Lake above the village of Klukwan. I shared more Thomas Bay stories, interviews, and experiences I'd compiled, as well as a handful of eerie accounts from other places in Southeast.

"You should consider writing a book about the Kóoshdaa Káa," Carlton suggested. The thought of taking on the subject was daunting. To this day many Southeast Alaskans believe in and fear the Kóoshdaa

Káa. For some even saying the name is bad luck, let alone talking about it. Even people who don't believe speak cautiously about the subject. I was worried about offending Tlingit people and, though I didn't consider myself a superstitious person, part of me was afraid. I was also fascinated though. With a heavy dread tinged with excitement, I thanked Carlton and told him I'd consider it.

I went home, googled "kushtaka," and found a few brief, vapid articles on Sheen's quest to find the Kóoshdaa Káa in the summer of 2013. There were also a few monster blogs, a Wikipedia article, and an episode of *Alaska Monsters*, a reality television show, called "The Otter-man." Try as I might, I was unable to resist spending three dollars to waste the next hour of my life watching a bunch of guys, who appeared to be taking a break from working in meth labs, shooting guns and raising a ruckus that seemed more like farm animals having an orgy in a slaughterhouse than a Kóoshdaa Káa "hunt." It was filmed in Wasilla, famous as the breeding grounds of the Palins, nearly 1,000 miles away from Southeast Alaska, where stories of the Kóoshdaa Káa come from. The monster hunters got a tip that the "Otterman" was frequenting a small lake which, conveniently, they were able to drive to. They had many run-ins with the creature and built a trap "combining cutting-edge technology and Native American spirituality." The show ends with the hunters trapping the Otterman, but then the fiend shape-shifted into fire and escaped. Memorable quotes include:

"We got thousands of people missing in this triangle. My thoughts is it could be the Otterman!"

"It's payback time! That rat bastard pulled me into the pond!"

"Otterman, you're going down!"

"Rat bastard. . . . We had the son of a bitch!"

"We have creatures out here that are dangerous beyond your imaginations."

The following morning I opened my e-mail to find another rejection letter from a publisher for a book on natural history I'd been working on for months. The editor's comments were heartbreakingly valid and thoughtful—nature, to most folks, is not sexy enough to justify paying $15 dollars only to be tortured and bored by stories of birds, bears, and earth-muffin reflections. I half considered a book project composed of all the rejections I'd received since I started writing. It could be akin in length and scope to Tolstoy's monster *War and Peace*. Maybe I'd call it *Failure and Rejection*. With a sort of giddy abandonment that comes with having nothing to lose, I fired off a couple queries to publishing agencies about a book on scary stories and mysteries of Southeast Alaska. Both wrote back immediately saying they wanted it. The next thing I knew I had a book deal.

What ensued was a strange journey, partly consisting of dialing up strangers in a number of Southeast communities and saying things like, "Hi, my name is Bjorn Dihle. I heard you had an . . . an . . . an experience with a Kóoshdaa Káa?"

More often than not, this was followed by an awkward silence, an apology, and frequently a good laugh once the person realized I wasn't a serial killer. Multiple folks said something along the lines of, "Nope, sorry, never have. If you hear of anything be sure to let me know." However, I dug deeper and more stories of encounters began to appear. What follows is a chronicle of something I gradually realized was much more complex than any other "boogeyman" I'd heard of.

Frederica de Laguna, a cultural anthropologist whose work *Under Mount Saint Elias: The History and Culture of the Yakutat Tlingit* is a valued ethnology of our region, recorded a number of Kóoshdaa Káa stories from the Yakutat area in the early 1950s: "Land otters (kucda), unlike ordinary animals, are really transformed persons," de Laguna wrote. "If, in theory, not all are such Land Otter Men (kucda-qa), yet the natives, even today, are ready to behave towards them as if they were. The land otter is more feared then [sic] the brown grizzly. The latter 'don't do nothing.' He only 'fights you,' and if you appeal to him for pity, he won't even 'bother you.' The land otter, however, is lurking to 'save,' that is, to capture those who drown, who are lost or who wander in the woods, and such unfortunates are taken by these Land Otter Men to their homes or dens, and unless rescued in time by a shaman are in their turn transformed into land otters."

George Thornton Emmons, a US Navy lieutenant stationed in Alaska during the late 1800s, wrote extensively of Tlingit culture. Toward the end of his life, at the request of the American Museum of Natural History, he began organizing decades of ethnographic notes. After his death, Frederica de Laguna spent thirty additional years editing Emmons's material before his respected book, *The Tlingit Indians,* was published in 1991. He wrote this about the Kóoshdaa Káa:

> Since cremation was not only a religious rite but a sacred duty, necessary to the happiness of the dead, drowning and the loss of the body was the most dreaded death. The body of the drowned, if not recovered, might be 'rescued' by the Land Otter People and would become a Koushta ka, or Land Otter Man. The transformation was slowly accomplished: first hair grew over the body, speech became confused, he began to walk on knees and elbows, a tail grew out, and, in time, he became more otter than human. Upon seeing anyone, he would try to be recognized and if so he would be saved. If his body was found and cremated he would be saved.

Kóoshdaa Káas are particularly drawn to children. Most often victims are snatched when they wander into the woods or near the water. A Tlingit friend of mine from high school became a little exasperated when I asked him what he thought about the scary stories.

"They're just old wives' tales that grandmas tell to keep kids from going off into the woods or near the ocean," he said.

Ethel Lund, an eighty-four-year-old Raven of the Kiks.ádi (Frog) clan and the Sun House, who helped found Southeast Alaska Regional Health Consortium (SEARHC), told me about the cautionary tales she heard growing up.

"I grew up in a Tlingit household and they used to threaten you if you didn't behave—a boogeyman that comes around. And then I saw these little otters, I don't know if that was what they were referring to. I never really grabbed on to that, but boy, I know some people who really do believe."

David Katzeek, whose Tlingit name is Kingeisti, an elder, leader, and Eagle of the Thunderbird clan of Klukwan, is not sure why the Kóoshdaa Káa is linked to the land otter. "It's kind of a mystery for me the reason why the land otter was selected," he said.

Many people think of the Kóoshdaa Káa as a furry demon running around in the woods or out in the ocean but Katzeek says it's much more complex.

"It's a spirit," David said. "You all know what a Kóoshdaa Káa is in one respect. There's not a person that doesn't experience it. It basically tries to steal your mind; tries to steal, in a way, your self-esteem. It takes away from you. It causes you to become a person you really were never intended to be. Like being an alcoholic; being a drug addict; a child abuser. The list goes on with respect to all the negative types of things. . . . Our thoughts become Kóoshdaa Káa type of thinking. There isn't anybody that doesn't have that kind of experience. What is a Kóoshdaa Káa in a way? It's spirit that basically says, 'Only if you're like me, then you're going to be okay.'"

Frank Katasse, an Eagle whose Tlingit name is Kaash, has been fascinated by the stories ever since he was a small child. He's now in his early thirties and a talented actor, playwright, and writer.

"The Kóoshdaa Káa in its form can be a whole bunch of things, whether it's a literal or figurative definition," Frank said. "It's just too unexplainable; too many weird things happen for it not to be. Maybe it's because the seed was planted, but I mean a lot of the stuff is too weird for it not to be real."

The Kóoshdaa Káa defies any Western system of classification—it's a monster, spirit, and a metaphor all at once. For many people in Southeast Alaska, even those educated by universities and firmly rooted in twenty-first-century technologies and customs, it's disturbingly real in both a spiritual and physical sense. At one point called "ghosts or revenants" by de Laguna, Kóoshdaa Káas actively hunt victims. They possess the ability to shape-shift, hypnotize, and often turn people at least temporarily insane. They frequently mimic the sound of a crying infant, or call out to their prey and appear as a deceased or living acquaintance of a loved one. All to lure their victims into the dark, sodden forest or onto the cold and stormy ocean. De Laguna wrote: "They (Land Otter Men) appear to him (victim) in the guise of his own relatives or friends, and the place to which they take him looks just like his own house. Here they offer him some of their food. But if he eats it, he can never come back to his own home again. He will go 'crazy' and become a land otter."

One man I interviewed, who wished to remain nameless, spoke of how a Kóoshdaa Káa often fixates on one person, usually a child, and tries repeatedly to catch or lure the child into the woods or out on the water. He learned this after making a rather eerie discovery in the woods near a village.

"What I found was under a tree in the woods were these clothes folded up. They looked like a young boy's clothes. They were all covered in moss so they'd been there for a long time. They were all folded neatly in place. It was explained to me, when I asked about it, to fool the Kóoshdaa Káa so that they think they've captured that person. So, you put the clothes there and they won't seek that person."

The people of Yakutat, whom de Laguna interviewed, told numerous stories of the obsession the Kóoshdaa Káa had with children. Children were told if someone approaches and wants to take them somewhere to "get a hold of their hand and bite. . . . If they were kucda-qa, their skin move like that [quivers], like live fish." A Kóoshdaa Káa was always suspected when children went missing. Searchers organized, preferably with dogs, and consulted a shaman. Emmons wrote that dogs offered protection against Kóoshdaa Káas, "because they were never fooled by the friendly appearance which these evil creatures might assume to lure intended victims." De Laguna speculated that some adults told children to defecate or urinate if they suspected a Kóoshdaa Káa was nearby. One story from Dry Bay relates a little boy being taken after a Kóoshdaa Káa appeared to him as his mother. When he urinated and defecated in the house he thought was his mother's, he realized he was in a den and frightened otters were running from him. Eventually his sister found him in a hole.

"They took him home to tie him up. Don't know what he's going to do," says de Laguna's transcription of the interviewee's story. "Just like he's crazy. He running for his own sister find him that family. 'Ixt' save him for him. (This seems to mean that they had to tie up the boy, who was crazy, and who was trying to run from his sister back to the land otters, not realizing that he was home safe, but thinking he still had to find his family.)"

Another story of a child being taken by a Kóoshdaa Káa posing as his mother was recorded by de Laguna:

> My father's oldest brother got captured by land otters out at Situk. He was about four years old. My mother told us, 'Don't go too far in the dark, in the night time.' . . . He was found two days later, caught between the roots of a tree. When he came to, it was dark, pouring down rain, and he had no clothes on or anything. . . . That Indian doctor's spirit caught him. He go under the trees. The kucda-qa drag him through the roots. They let him drop right between them. He pooped all over himself and they don't want to handle him. . . .

People, children and adults alike, who've encountered or are taken by the Kóoshdaa Káa frequently go insane and bringing them back into the community is difficult. De Laguna recorded a story about a girl that was brought back from the clutches of the Kóoshdaa Káa: "The girl had encountered Land Otter Men in the woods and returned half crazed and raging, she attacked everyone, struck and bit those who tried to hold her, and tearing off her clothes, ran around naked. . . . The description of the girl's frenzy corresponds with what Yakutat informants say about the behavior of persons who had been captured by land otters. . . . "

People who fell into the ocean or became lost in the woods were thought to be in danger of being taken by the Kóoshdaa Káa. Every year, for the past 10,000 years, numerous people vanish into the water and woods of Southeast Alaska. Dee Longenbaugh, owner of Observatory Books, was surprised by the honor of being adopted into a Tlingit clan during a potlatch in Yakutat nearly fifty years ago.

"Now, Kóoshdaa Káa, that is misinterpreted, badly misinterpreted by white people," she said. "The Kóoshdaa Káa is the land otter people. What they really are are people who are out in their boat and the boat sinks and they drown. They're not evil people that show up and run around and all sorts of awful things. . . . Now I will tell you a true story that was told to me as true and I believe it. It was either Angoon or Hoonah. . . . An older white man that lived outside the village for years and got along with everyone. In the fall, he heard a noise at his front door. He went to investigate and there was a young couple wearing rain gear and just dripping, it was really dripping and water just running off them. It was cold out and the old man asked them to come and warm themselves at the fire. They came a little closer, but still hung back. He offered them food and something to drink. They shook their heads no. The water kept dripping off them. The old man felt weirded out. The couple stayed for a while and then turned around and walked back out in the nasty weather. . . . The next morning the old man went into the village and told them what had happened and described the couple. An older woman burst into tears. She knew who that was. They went out the day before on a boat and hadn't come back. That's the real Kóoshdaa Káa."

Tara Neilson, a writer whose blog you can visit at alaskaforreal. com, lives in the wilds of Southeast Alaska aboard a float house. She grew up without a phone, still doesn't have one, and feels uncomfortable using one, so she wrote to me:

I can't actually remember the first time I heard about the

kushtaka. They always just seemed to be a given part of growing up in the wilderness. We lived in the ruins of a burned down cannery so it had this spooky, apocalyptic air; we had the sense that there were ghosts of the past all around. I think it was probably the fishermen in our family who talked about them and we just overheard the adults talking. Fishermen tend to be superstitious, in my experience, and they took the possibilities of kushtaka encounters while anchoring up in remote bays very seriously.

I can only say I had an impression that the fishermen thought of the kushtaka as a shape-shifter, an alien being with malicious intent, something extremely evil. I found this interesting, but only mildly scary. I felt it was possible that such evil existed, but it seemed to me that when I heard about something really bad happening, humans were doing it to each other. Usually influenced by the demon rum, a far more prevalent evil 'spirit.' I've known a lot of people who got a spooky feeling in the woods and they attributed it to kushtaka lurkers, but other than my sister, I never met anyone who said they'd actually seen one.

De Laguna received a letter in late December of 1955 telling of a big storm near Yakutat that caused two men to drown. Kóoshdaa Káas appeared in the area and tried to capture another man whose boat went down:

Big Bill E that lives across Ben T (near the head of Monti Bay) also capsized; was lost on his way to Yakutat from Situk. . . . Three days after the big storm, one of the boys, Butch, went out on his plane, searching, and saw him rolling around on the sandy beach of Point Manby. No skiff. Butch was landed by him and trying to help him up to the plane. Bill refused to go. He saw so many slim mans around him. He saw them himself. Those slim mens were talking excited. That was Land Otter Men. His story's so interesting. He saw pretty looking girl, too. He even see big truck come by to pick him up, but he refuses to go or refuse to talk to them. He even saw his skiff dry up and later smashed by the slim men. When he was picked up by plane, his skiff just disappeared.

I heard Gil S (another White man) saw the same things when his skiff capsized with him two summers ago. He saw a skiff rushing to him but didn't reach him. Only one big land otter there.

Looks like Bill is out of his mind when he was first brought out....

Kóoshdaa Káas are said to be responsible for causing natural disasters such as landslides and avalanches. A number of reports indicate that Thomas Bay, the setting of *The Strangest Story Ever Told,* experienced a massive landslide that wiped out a Tlingit village of 500 people a couple hundred years ago. Supposedly, a number of the victims became Kóoshdaa Káas. Ethel Lund remembers her uncle having a strange experience while hunting in Thomas Bay.

"I asked my uncle about it," Ethel said. "How did it feel? He said it's just like you're being watched but you never see anything."

A May 19, 1994, article in the *Petersburg Pilot* tells of a Tlingit hunter's encounter in Thomas Bay during the 1930s. Deep in the woods, the man "first heard a whistling sound and then someone calling his name as a bizarre feeling overtook him. Realizing that these were the signs of the Kushtakas, he did what he was told would bolster his strength against them. He grabbed a branch and bit down on it, as he nervously left the area. He was so rattled by the experience, he never hunted again...."

According to some, a person can do a number of things to deter the Kóoshdaa Káa. Dogs, urine, poop, metal (particularly copper), and tobacco are all types of protection. One older Tlingit woman suggested urinating in a circle and standing in it if you felt you were being stalked. In one village, I was informed by a man who wished to remain anonymous that many women, at least until fairly recent times, carried Bibles under their coats for protection. Properly disposing of clothing after an encounter with a Kóoshdaa Káa is also important.

Forty-five years ago, on a pleasant summer day, Carlton Smith hitched a ride on a gillnetter from Juneau up Lynn Canal to Haines just to enjoy the beauty of the mountains and ocean. While en route, near Lincoln Island, he was climbing down a ladder to the deck of the boat when it broke loose and flung him into the ocean. There was an intense eeriness to being underwater he'll never forget. When he popped up to the surface he saw the boat disappearing into the horizon. Luckily, the skipper soon realized his friend was absent and pulled a wide turn and plucked Carlton out of the frigid waters. A day or so later, back in Juneau, Carlton was approached by David Katzeek's mother. She demanded the clothes he'd been wearing when he fell into the water and then took them out to a point above the ocean and burned them so he'd no longer be marked by the Kóoshdaa Káa.

Some stories are humorous, as was the one Ethel Lund told of one of her grandfather's best friends.

"The kids came into the house and told them they saw a Kóoshdaa Káa out in the woods and they were very excited. We all heard about Kóoshdaa Káas as the boogeymen when we were kids. His wife was going up to the post office and said she'd be back in about an hour. 'Well, I'm going to go out to the smokehouse 'cause they got a hole in the back that I can see through and I can look at the woods where they saw the Kóoshdaa Káa.' So he parked himself there and was looking through the smoke hole and his wife came back from the post office. In those days, and I can remember when I was young, a great many Native women wore fur coats. She came home excited, wanting to show off her fur coat so she goes in the smokehouse and taps him on the shoulder and he turns around. . . ."

At that point in the story Ethel was laughing so hard that the rest of the telling was a pantomime indicating the husband, surprised and horrified, tried to flee so fast he ran into the wall of the smokehouse and knocked himself out.

David Katzeek told of an experience during a deer hunt he made with his father and brother-in-law.

"One November day, I had a nineteen-foot skiff with a ninety-horsepower Johnson outboard on it. I took my boat and my dad and brother-in-law down to a place across from Grand Island, just below Doty Cove. We call that one little mountain down there below Doty Cove the meat locker because basically, for whatever reason, they're always up around that little mountain. We always get our deer and everything else there . . . we just take what we need. We could have shot a lot of deer. It was around Thanksgiving. My dad always read the weather and he said, 'When the noon time comes, David, the weather is probably going to switch to north winds and we can't anchor down here. . . . Once you hear the wind begin to blow, you need to turn around and go back to the boat.'

"I took off and heard a shot and thought my dad had got one. So, instead of going into the woods, I walked all along the shore almost back up to Doty Cove. Then I hunted the ridge. . . . I just got up on the ledge and there was a big deer standing there. When it was jumping it sounded like sacks of flour hitting the ground, it sounded like a horse running. I yelled, 'HEY!' The deer stopped and looked back. . . . Boom, I hit it. It keeled over. When I started to gut it out I thought it was a big, big doe. But it was a buck after mating—a buck doesn't have any horns then. So, I was so happy. I gutted it. I didn't even have to walk very far. I brought the deer down and put it on a log. Then I started walking up that little ledge. . . . Boom, I got another one. There was not even a half hour, I had two. . . . So, I carry that one down and I go and walk another forty minutes or so and I shoot another one. I hear the wind blowing. . . .

"I start walking back to where we anchored the boat. My dad was wearing a red and black wool jacket. My brother-in-law was using the same kind of jacket except that it was green and black. I look up and they're sitting on a log smoking cigarettes and I wave at them. I scream real loud. They look up at me. . . . I yelled, 'I got three deer!' They just kept on smoking. I thought that's strange. So, I'm walking down and I looked up—I don't think it took me a minute or less—I looked up and they were gone. I said what the heck, where in the world? I just yelled, 'I just told you guys!' I yelled real loud, 'I just told you guys I got three deer!' So, I'm running along the beach. They were sitting by a log with a fifty-gallon drum that was rotting out from rust. I go over there and look. I don't really see anything. I know I saw them there. All of a sudden I want to catch up to them. I had such a compulsion. I was chasing after them, hollering and telling them I need your help. I have three deer. They were moving ahead of me. It was like a regular path. It was real clear and I was going and going. Suddenly I came up to a huge tree that had fallen down with its roots all spread out. I thought, what the heck am I doing? I looked around me and there was nothing but devil's club all around me where I thought I was running on a clear path. I got scared. I grew up in church so I started to pray. All that kind of stuff because I thought of Kóoshdaa Káa. I asked myself what did grandma tell you about Kóoshdaa Káa? What is a good repellent for Kóoshdaa Káa? What she said is the thing that the Kóoshdaa Káa hates the most, it cannot stand it, it will have to run, there's no way it's going to capture you. So, I said, 'What is it, Grandma?' She said you have to fart.

"So, you can see this twentieth-century Tlingit standing in the woods trying like hell to fart and I couldn't. When I went to the boat my dad and brother-in-law were there. They said, 'Where have you been?' I said, 'I've been calling you, I chased you guys.' They said, 'When?' I said, 'Just now.' My brother-in-law said, 'We've been here for the last forty-five minutes.' The waves were really big. We went over to Doty Cove and picked up my deer and went home."

The following weekend a boat, with a family aboard, iced up and sunk in stormy seas near Grand Island and Doty Cove. All were lost. David remembered, "It was sad. We could hear them on the radio telephone calling for help. Telling the Coast Guard they were going down. It was only one man and the rest were young ladies. I don't know whether that had anything to do with the Kóoshdaa Káa thing I saw. I could draw a picture of that real quick, really easy. There was something real I experienced. It wasn't just running through devil's club trying to catch up. . . . "

Years ago, Frank Katasse had a strange experience while camping with friends out by Peterson Creek north of Juneau. They were standing around a fire when they heard a sound like a high-pitched scream and the swoosh of wind pass between them.

"We were kind of laughing about it for a while when we were out there but then it became real serious," Frank remembered. The screaming and gust of movement continued periodically. "We thought that someone was running between us or something, but the fire was only two feet to our left."

Frank had brought along his brother's giant mellow dog. That night, it barked and growled constantly, like there was a bear nearby. Someone made the joke that it was probably just the Kóoshdaa Káa and at first the group chuckled, though nervously. Their laughter ended abruptly when the thing shrieking "went crazy."

"The consistency of it was what creeped us out," Frank said. "We were trying to find the logic in it all. It was just super weird."

The friends had had a few beers and didn't want to drive home, so they climbed into a tent and waited for daylight. Frank was so creeped out he slept in the car. All night long his dog stared out the window. "He'd just be sitting there looking out and growling like there was bear or something outside the door," Frank said. "I was super creeped out."

Many strange stories come from the woods and waters of Southeast Alaska. Sometimes people are struck with odd feelings, compulsions, and hallucinations. Other times, people hear, sense, or even see something they can't explain. Sometimes they're a mixture of both. The common thread most folks share is that they were unable to rationally explain what happened to them.

Mike Stedman, co-owner of Alaska Seaplanes, and his two sons, Jake and Matt, are hardworking and practical outdoorsmen. They're the sort of guys that look like they could suppress a prison riot. If, for some wild reason, Mike and a brown bear exchanged blows, I'm not sure who'd come out worse. They're also some of the most levelheaded people I've met, which makes the following story that much more eerie.

Mike used to frequently take his family to a cabin on Florence Lake, only accessible via floatplane, on the northwest side of Admiralty Island. In 2010, after the area had been logged, the Stedman family returned to the lake. The surrounding land had turned into brush so thick you could barely see your nose if you tried to wander through it. That evening, while Jake and Matt were out on the water fishing for cutthroat trout, Mike and his wife, Laurie, enjoyed a campfire. Jake's dog, Cedar, an easygoing English Labrador retriever, sat nearby. Suddenly a huge branch broke off from a tree and impaled the ground just yards away. A few moments later, Cedar went crazy barking at something nearby in the woods.

"Cedar ran around the side of the cabin barking . . . really barking like something was there," Mike remembered. "So, I grabbed the 7 mm [rifle] and went around the side of the cabin. She's barking and barking and barking. . . . My first thought is bear."

Admiralty Island, according to many folks, has just about the densest concentration of brown bears in the world. It's not uncommon that an inquisitive one will wander into camp. It was possible the last folks to use the cabin had been careless and taught a bear to associate people with food.

"Hey!" Mike yelled, hoping to scare off the bear or make it stand so he could see where it was.

"I'm over here!" a voice yelled back from nearby in the brush. Mike jacked a round into the chamber of his rifle as Cedar, shivering and pressed into his leg, went nuts. Mike hollered again, hoping to get the owner of the voice to show itself.

"She didn't quit barking for, I bet it was five minutes," Mike said. "Then she just stopped. Jake and Matt came back and were like, 'What the hell is going on?' They heard the dog barking and me yelling. Of course they didn't believe me."

Mike tried to come up with a rational explanation for the voice he heard. He considered state troopers, or folks off another floatplane, in the bushes and messing around. They hadn't heard another plane, though. Despite being logged, the area was very remote. There was a logging road that connected Florence Lake to Cube Cove and the coast, but that had become grown in with brush and is impossible to drive. The logging camp had been closed down and dismantled a decade prior. Unless there was a squatter hiding in the woods, there wasn't anyone who lived within at least thirty miles or more of the area. Mike read the cabin's log.

"There's other entries from like five guys out there," Mike said, "and they were afraid to get their beer because there was something out there."

Mike never said the word Kóoshdaa Káa, but I couldn't help but wonder as I listened to his story. One thing's for certain, Mike and Laurie won't spend the night at the Lake Florence cabin again.

"It's not just that," Mike said, ever practical, "but I think that tree is going to fall on the cabin."

It was either the next year or the following that Mike flew Jake, his wife, Rachel, and their toddler, Mara, to Lake Florence for the weekend. They made a plan for a pickup, said their good-byes, and Mike flew back to Juneau. Jake woke early the next morning to go fishing before breakfast, leaving Rachel and Mara asleep. He took the small skiff a mile or so from the cabin and then trolled for trout. An albino deer emerged from the brush and walked along the shore—a sight many outdoor folks in Southeast go their whole life without seeing. For an hour or so Jake enjoyed watching the deer, fishing, and the solitude of the quiet morning. He putted back to the cabin, tied the boat off, and looked up to see Rachel staring questioningly at him.

"What took you so long?" Rachel asked.

"What do you mean?" Jake asked.

"That wasn't you I was talking to?"

"Nope!"

Twenty minutes previously, Rachel and Mara had walked around the corner of the cabin. Mara wanted to see her dad and breakfast was ready. Rachel hollered out across the lake to let Jake know. A voice Rachel had assumed was her husband's called back from nearby. "I'll be right there!"

The couple examined the logbook. The last entry was from Jesse Walker, a master king salmon fisherman and a good friend, from three years ago. Walker has no recollection of anything weird happening while he was staying at the cabin, other than the cutthroat fishing being dynamite.

"There were a lot of spooky entries in the log," Jake said. There were accounts of people afraid to leave the cabin because of something outside. There was an account of hearing scratching on the wall. One group left their beer in a creek, only to have it stolen. Another party went for a hike, returned to the cabin, and found all their stuff removed from inside and placed on the porch.

Jake and Rachel aren't sure what to make of it, but Rachel is sure of one thing. She won't ever visit that lake again.

Both David Katzeek, a fluent Lingít speaker and Ethel Lund, a dormant Lingít speaker, expressed how invaluable the language is. David called the language "phenomenal" and "very precious." Ethel said part of the reason she learned the language was because she loves Tlingit jokes and they're not as funny in English. Much of the meaning and complexities of a story can't be expressed in English. Stories are easily misinterpreted or not fully appreciated when they've been translated. This has limited many people's understanding of what the Kóoshdaa Káa really is. It doesn't just live in the woods or ocean. According to David, it's in many of our homes.

"There's all kind of Kóoshdaa Káas," David said when I was sitting with him and Peter Metcalfe at T.K. Maguire's, a restaurant in Juneau. Peter, like Carlton Smith, had been a big help with story ideas and interviews. He was currently writing a biography of Ethel Lund and had published a number of books on Alaska Native history. David continued, "You're going to find it in resentment. Anger. Ego. Self-esteem will be part of it. . . . It's causing people to destroy the earth. If you see what people are doing to people. How they're treating other people because they don't look them, talk like them, smell like them, walk like them. . . . That's the spirit of the Kóoshdaa Káa. You're going to take them. You're going to capture them in a way to make them like you. To walk like you. Think like you. Talk like you. Act like you. Every human being has a Kóoshdaa Káa in him. This is not modern stuff I'm telling you. This is the ancient kind of stuff that the elders would bring to the table. That's the reason why I'm saying the elders, if they were sitting here, they would be nodding their heads up and down because all the stories have it in it. Here is the thing they wanted everyone to know: that there is a Kóoshdaa Káa and it does take possession of you. It can actually take possession of your soul."

David's voice echoed with so much power and emotion that the other restaurant patrons sat silently, listening. He shared a story from Klukwan, a Tlingit village located twenty-one miles up the Chilkat River from Haines. (If you've read John Muir's classic *Travels in Alaska,* you might recall him saying that the Chilkats were the most feared and revered group of Tlingits.) An hour and half later, when David finished, his lunch sat untouched and cold on his plate. I'll try to do the story some semblance of justice.

It began with a young orphan taken in by his uncle. The man loved his nephew and treated him kindly and with much affection. So much his wife grew envious and contemptuous of the boy. She wanted her husband to think only of her. She refused to give the boy good parts of salmon or deer to eat, and treated him poorly in other ways. One day, the uncle decided to go hunting even though his smokehouse and larder were full of fish and venison.

"Be good and kind to him," he told his wife. She nodded, but her body language betrayed her true feelings. When the man disappeared into the woods, the auntie sent the boy to the smokehouse to make sure there weren't any squirrels or ravens bothering the meat and to put some peeled alder to smoke on the coals. The smokehouse was full of fat salmon, deer, and seal.

"I wonder how come uncle is going hunting, he's got lots of food here," the boy said to himself, awed by the delicious meat smoking. He reached up

for a choice part of a salmon that he always imagined tasting. While he was chewing blissfully, lost in the flavor and texture, his auntie appeared in the doorway.

"What are you eating?" she asked, prying his mouth open, ripping out the food and sending the shocked boy to the house. She was overcome with a savage desire to hurt the boy. She placed a chunk of meat in boiling water, waited until it was scalding hot, and stuck it into the child's mouth.

At that point in the story, David asked: "Do you think there's things like that happening today? Yeah. This isn't 10,000 years ago or 1,000 years ago or some little creature running around on the riverbanks, on the streams and little ponds that's going to take you, that's going to catch you. Yes, they used that because it was really a creature that took possession of you. If I was telling this out at the place I teach, I would say, 'You see this?' The Kóoshdaa Káa spirit is right here right now with you and me. . . . When I see the news today, guys. When I hear we're bombing women and children because we need to be 'protected.' That we're really in danger. That is the spirit of the Kóoshdaa Káa. They're killing a lot of old men, old women, and babies. Why? Because of oil. In this world, here's what the elders would say, too: 'Can you see why our people are the way they are?' The Kóoshdaa Káa spirit wants to hear how he is. So, they're asking you about how the spirit of the Kóoshdaa Káa is. It likes to hear the negativity type of stuff. That's the monster."

The boy, his mouth seared, cried and called out for his uncle. Other people in the community heard his crying but they didn't want to get involved. The young boy's mouth was so burned, and he was in so much pain, that he snuck away, crawling on his belly into the bushes to hide. For how long he lay in the bushes no one knows, but eventually he crawled to a stream filled with salmon and began lapping up water. The spirit of the Kóoshdaa Káa came upon him and befriended him.

"So what do you think is broken in the person that is affected by Kóoshdaa Káa?" David asked. "Spirit. Trust. He don't trust anybody or anything. You can't trust even a higher power. You can't trust the spirit of God. That's not because you are bad. It's because of the experience that you've had with respect to those that you did trust or the one that you did trust."

The uncle returned from his hunt to find his wife alone. Knowing too well his wife's heart, he asked where his nephew was.

"I don't know. He just left," his wife said. The uncle and others in the community searched for the boy, but the Kóoshdaa Káa made him invisible. Eventually they gave up looking. The Kóoshdaa Káa took the boy deep into the woods. After awhile the boy began to like the different types of food he ate and the caves and dens he slept in. For a long while the Kóoshdaa Káa possessed him. One day it brought the boy to a place where a great waterfall came off the top of the mountain. Birds flew all over and water bursts sprayed the surrounding rocks and trees. The beauty of the place was so intense that for the first time in a long while he forgot what possessed him. He became aware of the beauty of the waterfall and multitudes of bird flying in every which direction. He felt the untrammeled earth. Below, salmon, trout, and steelhead filled a crystal clear stream. He became aware of creatures of the woods and mountains. Life that only a moment before he'd been too blind to see was everywhere. He became in tune with the earth and a greater power took possession of his being.

"That's a big word, Be-ING," David said. "We say human being. Tlingit people say Be-ING human. Being. You're being. It means you're not yesterday, you're not tomorrow, you're right now. I look at the way the elders say he drew the spirit from those things. I say the strength he had within him was brought out by acknowledgment of the strength of all the others. Our elders would say a long time ago: 'You have it in you.' What do you have? You have the strength, you have love, you have kindness, you have patience, you have understanding, you have intelligence, you have wisdom, you have courage, you have faith. But, you also have the bad things."

The boy stood high in the mountains, listening to the earth speak to him, and began to feel human again. He, like so many people alive in the world today, was once unable to hear the earth because the Kóoshdaa Káa had stopped his ears up. He was no longer a boy. Now a young man, he began descending the mountain's ancient trails back toward his uncle's village. He became aware of his strength and the earth's strength and how they were interconnected. He abandoned the Kóoshdaa Káa where it first came and took him.

David sees it as akin to the moment an alcoholic or drug addict faces their demon and says, "This is a bunch of bull. I don't need this anymore. I don't need this anymore! I don't know what I'm going to do but I'm going to turn from it. I don't need it."

The young man was determined to return to his uncle and the village. Along the way he killed a mountain goat and packed the meat, hide, and tallow. Everybody was happy to see him. Even his auntie, who burned his mouth, feigned excitement.

"I'm so happy you made it back," she said. The mountain goat had a lot of tallow, which was a coveted delicacy. The young man's auntie was greedy for it. The young man, being generous, gave her all she wanted. She melted it over a fire and ate ravenously of the grease until she was stuffed. Gradually, the tallow hardened inside of her and she broke in half.

Later, after lunch with Peter and David, I went to work at the mental health unit. The story gave me hope and I was left wishing I could somehow articulate it to patients, many of whom were suffering mental illnesses at least partially rooted in, or exacerbated by, abuse by people they should have been able to trust the most. However, telling a Kóoshdaa Káa story to people experiencing psychotic breakdowns and delusions seemed like it might backfire. Pills were safer. Late that night, as I tried not to listen to a man scream about Hitler, I was left wondering about the power of narrative. The stories we tell determine the way we think of our lives. I'm convinced there's a story, that if told correctly, has the power to prevent people from becoming lost. The man screamed again, then laughed at his reflection in the mirror.

I've come to understand the Kóoshdaa Káa as a living metaphor, one that can exist both inside a person and in the rain forest and wild ocean passages. It offers fundamental lessons in being human and living in Southeast Alaska. As Frank Katasse said: "I think all Kóoshdaa Káa stories could be used as teachable moments for people to understand, which is kind of a very Tlingit way to do things. I don't know if I'll use it as much as it was used in the past. You know like 'Don't go wander in the woods by yourself or a Kóoshdaa Káa will get you.' There's some logic behind it there. So if it's a manifestation of your imagination or an actual thing, I don't think really matters."

At the end of our conversation, Frank held up a penny and teased that I should keep a bit of copper on me during future interviews. I chuckled, but both of us knew we were only half kidding.

9.

THE LEGENDS OF
THOMAS BAY

MORE than a half century ago, Virginia Colp came across a manuscript her deceased father had written. The story described events she'd only heard whispers of—a futile search for gold near Petersburg that led to madness, encounters with monsters, and the disappearance of men. Virginia had it published under the title *The Strangest Story Ever Told*. Now, it's likely the best-known scary story in Southeast Alaska.

In 2012, more than 100 years after the events in the book took place, two friends and I would venture into the bay in search of what we could find for ourselves. But first, here is a bit about the "strangest story" itself. Harry D. Colp, the author, is remembered by some old-time Petersburg residents as having a propensity for the bottle and barroom talk. Most residents shrug and smile when asked about Colp. His narrative centers around Thomas Bay, a quiet harbor ten miles east of Petersburg, across Frederick Sound, on the mainland. There is an unverified account of a massive landslide there that wiped out a large Tlingit village shortly before Russian fur traders ventured into the region. Some say the bay is haunted by Kóoshdaa Káas.

The Strangest Story Ever Told begins in 1900, a few years after 100,000 or more men and women flooded the north during the Klondike gold rush. A very small percent profited, many died, and the majority returned dejected to the Lower 48. Those who remained worked as miners, fishermen, and loggers. Colp, broke and in the company of three partners living in a shack, was residing in Wrangell when the story begins. One partner, whom Colp dubbed "Charlie," pestered "an old Tlingit man" about where he'd found a piece of quartz flecked with gold. The old man reluctantly gave Charlie directions to a supposed mother lode in the woods surrounding Thomas Bay. As soon as he could get an outfit together, Charlie paddled a canoe north toward the bay. He passed through the massive, silty Stikine River Delta, beneath the Horn Cliffs where sea lions bellowed from rookeries, and then turned into the steel-colored waters of Thomas Bay. A glacier crept into the ocean, and mountains and forest rose into clouds. He paddled to the southern end of the bay, thinking of how the old man had described finding gold above a lake shaped like a half-moon. He waited for high tide to cover an expansive tidal flat, then hauled his outfit to the forest's edge near the banks of the Patterson River. Weeks later, he showed up in Wrangell, looking like he'd been through hell, with only one piece of quartz freckled with gold in his boat. The night before boarding a ship to Seattle and leaving Alaska forever, Charlie told Colp and two other friends what had happened after he'd found the half-moon lake and the piece of quartz:

> Swarming up the ridge toward me from the lake were the most horrible creatures. I couldn't call them anything but devils, as they were neither men nor monkeys—yet looked like both. They were entirely sexless, their bodies covered with long coarse hair except where scabs and running sores had replaced it. Each one seemed to be reaching out for me and striving to be the first to get me. The air was full of their cries and the

stench from their sores and bodies made me faint. I forgot my broken gun and tried to use it on the first ones, and then I threw it at them and turned and ran. God, how I did run! I could feel their hot breath on my back. Their long claw-like fingers scraped my back. The smell from their steaming, stinking bodies was making me sick; while the noises they made, yelling, screaming and breathing, drove me mad. Reason left me. How I reached the canoe or hung on to that piece of quartz is a mystery to me.

I grew up terrified of the Kóoshdaa Káa and Thomas Bay, which is located a mere seventy miles south of Juneau. After I found out about them, I didn't sleep for days. The dark rain forest I lived at the edge of suddenly seemed haunted, but all the more enticing. I listened eagerly to secondhand stories of strange encounters in Thomas Bay. Rocks being hurled all night at an anchored boat; ominous footprints appearing in the snow; land otters shape-shifting into devilish creatures. In 2012, with two friends, I organized a trip to Thomas Bay to retrace the different routes Colp described prospectors taking in their search for the mother lode. On a dark and stormy day in early May, as the wind howled, trees moaned, and a violent outburst of sideways rain sounded like it might shatter a window, I rushed about packing so I could make the ferry that left Juneau that evening bound for Petersburg. My friend Ben M. and I had been talking about making a trip to Thomas Bay since we were teenagers. Like me, he was fascinated by *The Strangest Story Ever Told*. The phone rang. Ben's voice sounded hesitant and filled with trepidation.

"Five days in Thomas Bay gives us a really good chance," he said.

"Chance to?" I asked.

"You know," he said, his voice quietly trailing off. We debated what sort of protection we should bring for bears.

"I think I'm just going to pack my shotgun, if that's all right? You'd need a lot of practice before you could hit anything with my .44," I said.

"That's fine. I'll just use my bare hands against the little furry guys. I'll get a can of bear spray for the big furry guys," Ben said.

A few hours later, I boarded the *Malaspina* ferry and, against twenty-five-knot winds and rain, motored south toward Petersburg. That night I lay listening to the wind and ocean, dreamily wondering if this trip was a bad idea. My family had cautioned me; none of them necessarily believed in the Kóoshdaa Káa, but they didn't entirely disbelieve. Messing with such a dark concept seemed like it could have consequences. I assured them this undertaking was more of an investigation into human psychology, our relationship with nature, and what inspires our mythologies than a hunt for a forest demon. Our monsters, after all, tell us as much about ourselves as do our heroes.

The following dawn, sodden clouds rippled across the black mountains of Mitkof Island and Kupreanof Island. Houses, stores, boatyards, and marinas rose out of the gloom. A few days prior, during high winds and big tides, the 408-foot *Malaspina* ferry slammed into the Ocean Beauty cannery. The ferry was fine, but the cannery didn't fare as well. Beyond the wreckage and the pier, a fleet of fishing and sport boats bobbed idly against buoy-padded docks. My friend Ben C. picked me up at the terminal. I agreed to help him with boat projects for a few days before heading out to Thomas Bay.

"Cup of coffee, then I'm putting you to work," Ben said as we threw my gear in the fish hold of the *Ouzel*, the thirty-one-foot boat he was leasing for the season. Between mounting the cross truss and trolling pole brackets, we made numerous trips to the town's two hardware stores.

"These bullets are five dollars cheaper at Walmart," a visiting bear hunter dressed in full camouflage told the clerk. A local danced the grapevine past us down Sing Lee Alley, once famous for its red-light district. The alley was named after Sing Lee, a Chinese merchant who was mysteriously murdered in 1932.

"I want what he's on," an old lady hollered beneath a dripping awning. Despite the steady downpour, a buzz radiated throughout the marinas and town. Men and women worked tirelessly on their boats, getting ready to gillnet, seine, and troll for salmon soon to return to inside waters. Black cod and halibut longliners were already braving the nasty waters to catch their annual quotas. Millions of dollars, all earned from the slime, blood, and hard work of fishing, floods through the community of 3,000 folks each year.

The weather broke a day after Ben M. flew in. We motored through the stiff currents of the Wrangell Narrows and out into the lumpy chop of Frederick Sound. Sea lions and cormorants rested atop red buoys. Dark spruce- and hemlock-clad mountain slopes rose into the snowy alpine. Three hours later we entered Thomas Bay and stared at thick clouds hanging heavily on the Baird Glacier, one of the few coastal glaciers still growing. The ocean seemed devoid of life. Only a loon interrupted the monotony of gray water. We tried to ignore two barges, buildings, trucks, and a logging road a few miles away from where we anchored. We paddled our inflatable rafts toward the Patterson River's expansive tidal flat. A hulking rust-colored beast prowled the forest's shadows.

"Holy cow! That brown bear is huge!" Ben M. said. We walked close together, me gripping my shotgun in one hand and carrying the raft in the other. After a few moments I realized the creature was not a bear. It was the likes of something I'd never seen in the wilds of Southeast.

"It's a cow," I said.

"A cow of a sow?" Ben C. asked.

"No, a cow," I said.

"Like, a cow of a bear?" Ben M. asked.

"No, a cow," I said.

"A cow moose?" Ben C. asked.

"No, like a dairy cow," I said. The guys scratched their heads in confusion.

"This is very strange," Ben M. said. Canadian geese flew overhead, their honking echoing deep within the forest. We carefully edged past the cow and walked along the Patterson River trying to scout a route to a mountain and the half-moon lake Colp had described. That night aboard the *Ouzel* we read through route descriptions in *The Strangest Story Ever Told*.

"This is it," Ben M. said, slamming his finger down on a mountain on the map. "We'll follow this logging road six miles, then head up the ridge and should be able to sight the half-moon lake from high up."

Early in the morning we paddled to shore beneath blue sky. Most of the Patterson and Muddy River Valleys had been logged between the 1940s and 1970s, somewhat compromising the mysteriousness of our venture. Less than a mile up the well maintained logging road we heard the buzz and roar of heavy machinery working. I walked up to a man operating a backhoe. Other machinery was at work in the background. He didn't seem surprised to see us.

"You can follow this road a good four or five more miles," he said. "There's some moose hunting camps along the way."

"Are you guys barging ore out of here to be processed elsewhere?" I asked.

"Nah. All the gravel for roads in Petersburg and communities on Prince of Wales Island comes from here. Their rock is too sharp and hard on their tires."

We followed the road through second growth forest until we got to the base of the mountain. A mangy deer bolted as we pulled ourselves up the steep and brushy ridge.

"Guys!" Ben C. called from a ledge. "I found something!"

We hurried over to where he stood holding a small piece of quartz flecked with what looked like gold.

"Just like in the story," Ben M. said, glancing around nervously. The first encounter in the narrative happened shortly after a prospector found a large piece of quartz flecked with gold on a mountain ledge.

We continued to the crest of the ridge and were awarded with a stunning view of the Patterson Glacier and the Devil's Thumb, a 9,000-foot-tall granite spire. Postholing through wet and rotten snow, we continued to the top of the mountain. We matched our landmarks with those described in Colp's narrative, and saw a lake shaped like a half-moon 2,500 feet below.

"Maybe it was in those flats next to the lake where John found Fred gnawing on saplings and barking like a dog," Ben M. said. The majority of weird accounts—people becoming irate, barking like dogs, losing track of time for weeks, and being stalked by devil creatures—happened in sight of the half-moon lake. With the pleasant weather and impressive views, we were having a hard time convincing ourselves there was anything supernatural and ominous about this place. Hours after leaving the summit we wandered through the stumps and brush of an old clear-cut.

"We're lost in devils' country," I said.

"We know exactly where we are. The road's that way," Ben C. said, pointing.

"I know," I said. "I've just been waiting all day to say that."

"A lot of stuff Colp wrote doesn't add up," Ben C. said an hour later when we stumbled out onto the logging road.

"He never claims to have seen any creatures and he didn't go crazy," I said. "I've been trying to think of an explanation other than the stories being a bunch of hype. I don't get a weird feeling from this place."

"The eeriest I felt was when we got into this logging area. The tone of forest totally changed. It became much darker . . . angry," Ben C. said. The other Ben and I agreed.

We started listing rational explanations for the legend and came up with several possibilities. Mental illness and the power of suggestion; chemicals leaching into drinking water; gases emitted from the earth that caused insanity and hallucinations; or maybe, just a chance to tell a good tall tale. I knew there was way more going on in the woods than I was conscious of. If I was alone and the weather was nasty it would be pretty easy to believe there was a malevolent force here. Later, in Petersburg, we'd hear rumors that there were high levels of arsenic in some of the creeks surrounding the bay. Arsenic poisoning can cause a variety of unpleasant symptoms, including confusion, paranoia, and hallucinations.

Reluctantly, we got back to our feet and slogged out to the beach as the sun sunk behind a mountain. We spent three more soggy days exploring without any strange encounters. However, I did fall into the ocean while attempting to get into an inflatable boat from the *Ouzel*. Afterward, Ben described me looking like a seal doing a graceful dive, but he was all business when he hauled me back aboard.

"Take your clothes off!" he screamed, shaking my shoulders before beginning to yank at my fleece. "Take your clothes off! We need to go skin to skin!"

"I think I'm okay, but thanks," I said, trying to back away. You can't get too far on a thirty-one-foot boat.

"Dammit, you're acting irrational!" Ben M. yelled, following me around. "Take your clothes off!"

Before heading back to Petersburg, we trolled for king salmon along the Horn Cliffs. It was here that a prospector claimed to shoot a devil creature that had been sitting on the bow of his canoe, cursing him all night whenever he'd taken a break from paddling. I looked up at a waterfall cascading thousands of feet down the cliff, bald eagles and red-tailed hawks circling above. Sea lions eyed us lazily as we trolled by.

"Dinner!" Ben C. cried as he reeled in the first king salmon of the year. Little Norway, a Petersburg celebration in honor of the 1817 signing of the Norwegian constitution, was in full swing when we got back to town. Vikings and Valkyries, wearing only wolf and grizzly bear skins, stormed the streets with broadswords, maces, and battle-axes. The more civilized members of the community strolled about wearing traditional Norwegian dresses, knickers, bonnets, and sweaters. Meghan, my five-foot-tall sister-in-law from Newfoundland, almost got in a fight with two ax-wielding brutes who tried to cheat at the herring toss competition. Naturally, with her seafaring history, she put them to shame and set a new Little Norway record for distance and accuracy.

"By Odin's beard! No one's ever got the herring in the bucket from that distance!" a Viking exclaimed, shaking his head in disbelief and then somewhat sheepishly hitting on her. We feasted on all you can eat shrimp, salmon and halibut buffets and drank like we'd died and gone to Valhalla. In the evening, I stood outside the Harbor Bar talking to my girlfriend on my phone, letting her know I'd survived devils' country.

"Are you talking to a girl!?" three giant, wolf pelt–clad Vikings yelled as they began to dry-hump me back and forth between them. "Huh? Are you?"

"I'm talking to my brother Olaf!" I said, trying to stay on my feet.

"Oh, sorry," one said, chagrined. They walked toward the bar's entrance, then stopped and looked back, unsure. "Is your brother's name really Olaf?"

"No," I said. They raised their broadswords to attack. "But I am Bjorn, the berserker!"

"By Thor's hammer!" They saluted and the four of us stumbled into the bar. A Viking with a mohawk climbed atop a table and a Valkyrie passed him a helmet full of beer. Other Vikings filled their helmets, too. An apple martini and a can of Rainier inexplicably found their way into my hands.

"To our fallen Viking brothers! To our fallen fishermen brothers!" The Viking with the mohawk bellowed, guzzled beer from the helmet, then dumped the rest over his head. The Vikings roared, drank, and saturated themselves with suds. I dumped the apple martini on my head and drank the beer. The ear-shattering thrum of techno filled the bar, and the fully armed barbarians, many with GoPros strapped to the tips of their swords, began to dance wildly. At three in the morning I stumbled back to the *Ouzel* and untied the boat as Ben C. fired up the engine. We lost Ben M. to his wife, who'd flown down to Petersburg when she found out what we were up to. We were on our way back to Juneau.

"Little Norway was much stranger than Thomas Bay," Ben hollered over the roar of the diesel engine.

"Loki's lute, we barely got out alive!" I yelled back. Thick mist hung on the mountains and the ocean lay flat as we motored past the dark and silent forest surrounding Thomas Bay.

I wrote the piece above shortly after the expedition, and then let it lie dormant. In 2015, my girlfriend, MC, was filling in as the editor for the *Capital City Weekly*, a newspaper for all of Southeast Alaska. She didn't have any stories, and had a fast-approaching deadline. Being a SNAG (sensitive new age guy), I dug into my dung heap of forgotten and rejected writing and found the Thomas Bay piece. It was published and to my somewhat surprise, blew up. I was contacted by numerous people. Some wanted to thank me for an interesting read. Others wanted to share their stories of Thomas Bay. One lady told of Czech miners in the bay who went insane and hid out in a cave sometime before World War II. A television producer called, curious about developing a reality show. Having worked on a handful of these silly productions as a guide, packer, and safety coordinator, I wasn't too helpful. Carlton Smith, a successful owner of a real estate company, suggested writing a book about the Kóoshdaa Káa. His suggestion was the genesis for *Haunted Inside Passage*.

Tara Neilson, a talented writer, who lives on a float house in the wilderness south of Wrangell and north of Ketchikan, also contacted me. She wrote, "I grew up out in the remote bush in an abandoned, partially burned down cannery and oh, yes, were we ever terrified of the kushtakas lurking out there!" Tara blogs at alaskaforreal.com, where she documents a wide array of subjects concerning Southeast Alaska. Relatively skeptical of supernatural explanations, Tara spent a lot of time researching possible explanations for the legends of Thomas Bay and Kóoshdaa Káas. One theory she heard at a dinner came from a man who grew up in Thomas Bay. He speculated the "devil creatures" featured in Colp's narrative might have been the Chinese survivors of a shipwreck who'd gone mad and become physically distorted from trying to stay alive in the wilderness. It's believed a ship carrying Chinese people to work in the canneries went down near Thomas Bay a few years before Colp and his partners began prospecting the area. One of Southeast Alaska's more forgotten histories is of the Chinese and other Asian people who worked the mines and canneries and built the roads and railways.

Another idea Tara put forward was that the legend may have been inspired from first contact with white explorers. Some theorize that Sir Francis Drake, the Elizabethan sea captain and knight, explored the Pacific Northwest but never made the venture public knowledge. Tara writes, "There are various essays by respected historians who . . . speculated . . . that he was on a secret mission by Elizabeth I to find the Northwest Passage, or Strait of Anian, as it was called." If this were the case he may have abducted Natives to serve as pilots through different channels and waterways. What happened to abductees after they served their navigational purposes can at best be speculated. There's a decent chance that they, one way or another, did not make it back to their villages. Drake and his crew, hairy and strangely dressed, must have appeared peculiar-looking at best. Perhaps some of the sailors remained behind and their odd, often menacing behavior toward Natives perpetuated stories of the Kóoshdaa Káa.

I began to research the legend more rigorously. I called around Petersburg and tried, unsuccessfully, to connect with descendants of Harry D. Colp. I chased rumors, most often coming up with nothing. A friend told me of an individual that had an odd encounter in Thomas Bay. When I finally got a hold of the man, he seemed a little confused.

"Nope. Far as I remember nothing weird has ever happened to me in Thomas Bay," he said. Soon we were both laughing. "But let me know if you find anything. It sure is a good story."

Another man, who owns a small logging company, and grew up in Thomas Bay, said he never ran across anything but admitted to being creeped out from the stories. Some old-timers, rumored to have had encounters, had passed on, taking their stories with them. I contacted Nancy Strand, a Southeast historian, and she told me the following story.

In the early 1960s, shortly after Alaska became a state, a stranger knocked at Nancy's door. This was Petersburg, a small, rough yet friendly fishing village full of salty Norwegians. Surrounded by dark rain forest and dangerous seas, hard men and women toiled to make their livelihood from the wilderness. Many hugged their families good-bye in the spring, boarded commercial fishing boats, and were away until the following winter. Others moved from one logging camp to the next. A few chased dreams of gold, but they were the less pragmatic members of the community. The stranger didn't look like a fisherman, logger, or prospector. Nonetheless, Nancy's father, Erling, invited him into their living room. A commercial fisherman, who drift-netted salmon on the nearby Stikine River, Erling served on the newly formed Board of Fish and Game. More than a half century later, Nancy's recollection of the interaction is still clear.

"I remember the man wearing a hat like Indiana Jones and asking Daddy questions about them [Kóoshdaa Káas]. Most specifically, he wanted to know if he needed any special permit to capture or shoot one. Daddy told him that he didn't think any permits were required. He told him Mr. Colp liked his whiskey and a good story."

Like Colp, most Alaskans enjoy whiskey and a good story, and consider it a crime to let the truth get in the way of an interesting tale. Whether the events described in the stories Colp left behind are true matters as much to me as why it still resonates so strongly. In the 115 years that have passed, logging operations, roads, a gravel quarry, and dairy farms have changed Thomas Bay. Small cruise ships regularly anchor in its protected waters, and guides lead tourists on short walks up Cascade Creek near an idyllic Forest Service cabin. Yet *The Strangest Story Ever Told* is still fascinating and scary. Perhaps it reconnects us, if only for a moment, with something primal, magical, and horrifying—an ancient sense of reality that's become so rare it's a treasure of sort. No matter how vivid Colp's imagination was, I can't shake the notion he seemed to believe what he wrote. Irving Warner, a Washington writer, interviewed Virginia in 1974 and stated that "she [Virginia] had confidence in her father's abilities and truthfulness." Ralph Young, an iconic Southeast character and bear guide, claimed Colp seemed as sane as anyone and that Colp appeared to truly believe his stories.

Harry D. Colp was seventeen when he caught the steamer *Derigo* from Seattle and came north in November of 1898, according to a

March 12, 1957, article in the *Petersburg Press*. The mass hysteria of the Klondike gold rush was petering out. Hardened men and women were returning south, poorer in pocket but, perhaps, richer in experience. Some who remained had fallen in love with the northern frontier. Others were half mad with gold lust, abandoning their diggings at the slightest whisper of a new strike. Dance hall queens and merchants followed in their wake. Boomtowns turned to ghost towns overnight. Those consumed by the quest to find gold worked their way west, prospecting different tributaries of the Yukon River, until they reached the Bering Sea and the city of Nome. There, some say, the spirit of the Klondike gave its last gasp and dissipated into the howling wind and pounding ocean.

Colp didn't follow the masses north. Instead, for reasons I can only guess at, he disembarked at Wrangell. The Stikine gold rush had long since ended and Wrangell, according to John Muir (I'm paraphrasing here), was kind of a pooh-pooh stain on the surrounding wilderness. Colp worked at a sawmill, transported mail to Kake, deckhanded on halibut boats and steamships, and prospected. In 1900 he formed a partnership with three other men. They were broke and ready to stampede at the next whisper of gold, no matter the consequences. The *Petersburg Press* reports, "Colp had first heard the story of the strangeness of the Devil's Thumb country from an Indian who came into Wrangell with stories of devils and spirits inhabiting the area. A gold specimen brought out by the Indian inspired Colp and some of his friends to go into the country."

The country the Tlingit man described was Thomas Bay, a place where Nancy Strand says Tlingit folks, at least formerly, didn't like to visit. Two of the four prospectors claimed to have encountered "devil creatures," that "were neither man nor monkey—yet looked like both." At least one went temporarily insane, barking like a dog on his hands and knees and convinced that "devils" were "trying to scare and fool me." The same man claimed that, after he and his partner had abandoned their outfit and fled Thomas Bay, a creature sat on the bow of his boat and cursed him every time he stopped rowing. Both men left for the south right afterward, supposedly never to return to Alaska. Colp's other partner did not see any creatures, but was quite disturbed by their partners' behavior. Colp and the unnamed man went into the bay early that September to salvage their outfit. He describes the setting as beautiful but a little eerie. "I felt as if we were the only living things in the big expanse of water and land."

In 1906 Colp tried to build a sawmill near Thomas Bay, in Brown Cove, and log parts of the Muddy River watershed. The venture was unsuccessful, but before leaving he ventured deep into that country and made a most surprising discovery. The March 22, 1957, article in the *Petersburg Press* read:

> When getting 28 miles inland from the mouth of the river they [Colp and his partner Johnny Sales] came upon a place where indications showed that there had been a complete settlement of Chinese working the soil for gold about 50 to 75 years prior. Tools, which were hand made, were found and it wasn't difficult to find the place where they had been washing the soil for gold, having done a great deal of digging. The place where the Chinese camp had been was along side of a glacier deposit and valuables had been taken from this place as no traces of gold were found. The Chinese had done a good job.

The Strangest Story Ever Told ends with a trapper disappearing along the Muddy River. One night during a snowstorm the trapper's dog began running around barking and howling. In the morning it was nowhere to be seen. The trapper followed the dog's trail and soon came across strange tracks that appeared to have been chasing his canine companion. The hind prints "were about seven inches long and looked as if they were a cross between a two-year-old bear and a small barefooted man's tracks. . . . The front set looked like a big raccoon's tracks, only larger . . . the creature could and did walk sometimes on all fours and at times on its hind legs."

The dog's tracks vanished mid-stride, much like those of a leaping snowshoe hare snatched in a wolf's jaws. The trapper followed the mysterious creature's trail, so "he might get a chance to shoot it and see what kind of animal it was." The tracks made a wide circle—it soon became apparent the thing was stalking the man. Horrified, the trapper left the area and reported the incident to a dairy farmer in Brown Cove. A short time later, after returning to his trapline, the man disappeared.

Between 1900 and 1911, Colp made a number of trips into Thomas Bay in search of gold. He was never able to stay long because his partners "became frightened by strange characteristics and tales of the country and refused to stay." He didn't find much gold nor did he suffer any madness or encounters with "devil creatures," though some of his partners on later expeditions did. Colp spent the next decade of his life prospecting and selling mining claims in different parts of Southeast. One colorful story relates an experience he and a partner had with inquisitive brown bears in the forests of Baranof Island. The two apparently didn't have a firearm, so they readied sticks of dynamite in case the animals attacked. From around 1917 to 1926, Colp homesteaded with his family at 5 Mile Creek on Kupreanof Island. He farmed foxes and fished for halibut. One old-timer remembers that Colp used to fish halibut with a hand-line "tied from the home to Sukoi island with hooks every few feet. He would start at one end and with a skiff, lift the line as he pulled himself along taking off the fish and rebaiting the hooks all the way to the island." Colp also worked as a skipper on a commercial shrimp boat and was known as "The Deacon" amongst the fleet. A tough, able, and industrious man, Colp embodied the spirit of old Alaska. He died in 1950 and took with him a whole pile of stories I wish I could have heard.

Nancy Strand never did find out if the would-be Kóoshdaa Káa hunter that visited her house when she was a teenager made it to Thomas Bay. He wasn't the first nor will he be the last to feel inspired to make the journey. The first documentation of an expedition inspired by the legends of Thomas Bay consisted of four men, led by US Commissioner Carroll Clausen of Petersburg in 1932. This was in the days before searching for the Kóoshdaa Káa was political suicide or anything to be ridiculed. Rumors exist that Theodore Roosevelt avidly hunted Bigfoot and a secret trophy room in the White House contains all sorts of stuffed cryptids. In 2016, I invited Hillary Clinton and Donald Trump to join me on a foray to Thomas Bay but never heard back. Clausen and his men said they were going to Thomas Bay for geographical reasons and to do a little prospecting. The *Petersburg Press* reported:

> Many hair-raising tales of the urchins and queer people in the 'Devil's Country' seem to bear little truth from the stories told by these men who spent all their time in and about the Half-Moon lake where great quantities of gold are supposed to have been found. Absolutely no trace of gold was found on this trip, however the party of men returned to Petersburg greatly satisfied in having made the trip being more familiar with the lay of the land and not half as willing to believe the tales of the large deposits of mineral, other than granite, which might be found in 'them thar hills' commonly known as Devil's Country.

The next expedition I know of, though I'm sure there were others, occurred around 1961. My good friend Joe Craig grew up chasing gold all over Southeast Alaska with his family. They lived on the M/V *Denali*, a wooden yacht that Al Capone had had built. Joe spent forty-two years commercial fishing, power trolling for salmon and longlining for halibut. When I mentioned to him that two friends and I were going to check out Thomas Bay, Joe told me the following story.

"When I was a kid, about eight or so, my family took our boat to Thomas Bay. We had all read the book and my father was an avid prospector and he wanted to find the gold deposit. So we get there and discover it's a %$*^@$# logging camp! Skiffs zooming around, lots of noise, etc. Anyway the next day we all went hiking, armed to the teeth—only thing we were lacking was some rocket-propelled grenades—and got quite a ways up the valley. Saw most of the landmarks described in the book but no ledge of gold. Actually the valley was quite peaceful, all in all. Knowing you, though, I imagine you'll have hand-to-hand combat with the little furry guys."

In 1978 Steve Atterton generated a lot of press when he decided to organize a massive expedition into Thomas Bay. Tree Top and Coleman were two of the corporate sponsors. The *Seattle Post-Intelligencer* reported Atterton planned to lead nearly two dozen scientists to investigate reports of strange creatures haunting Thomas Bay. Atterton came to Petersburg to ask the Forest Service about what sort of permit might be required for the expedition. Officials deemed none were needed. Virginia Colp, for one, did not approve. By that time she was getting sick of all the hype the book had generated. The *Petersburg Pilot* reported:

> Virginia Colp, daughter of the author of the book that was the catalysis for the expedition, wrote to the photographer Mike Siegrist and explained that 'she thought the whole idea was foolish.' According to Colp's printed statements she indicated that Thomas Bay was no longer a primitive area, and it did not need exploring. Colp also said that she had been approached by two different film companies to do a film which would make use of her father's book for material. Colp refused the companies the right to use the book in their productions.

The Atterton expedition was foiled by a lack of funding. Atterton claimed it would be postponed until the following year when enough money had been secured. The expedition never happened. Atterton, who now works as a party photographer in Las Vegas, looks back on that time period fondly.

A year after I explored Thomas Bay, Charlie Sheen chartered his private jet to Southeast Alaska. Apparently Sheen found a copy of *The Strangest Story Ever Told* and decided to mount his own investigation. The expedition is said to have occurred shortly after he finished looking, unsuccessfully, for the Loch Ness Monster. He didn't reveal many details to the media other than saying he read about Kóoshdaa Káas, became fascinated, and took his jet to Alaska to search for them. I called his agent to get more details but have yet to hear back.

10.

THE SINKING OF THE
ISLANDER AND THE LEGEND
OF ITS LOST GOLD

S OME say the ocean around Southeast Alaska is
haunted, and on quiet days you can hear the voices of
those who were lost at sea. Maybe these voices are just the result of the
odd way sound carries across the water, maybe they're Kóoshdaa Káas,
or maybe water is a living thing possessing memory. Growing up and
living in Southeast, you feel the danger of the ocean viscerally. There's
nothing irrational about this fear; locals all know people lost at sea. The
exact number of boats that have gone down can only be speculated, but
it's likely in the thousands. The sinking of the SS *Islander* was one of the
more famous tragedies.

In mid-August of 1901, the *Islander*, a 240-foot luxury steamer
deemed "unsinkable" and designed specifically for the Inside Passage, set
sail from Skagway. It was the apex steamer of Southeast Alaska and a veteran of the region's stormy and tricky passages. (In January of 1893, eight
years previously, the *Islander* had celebrated its thousandth voyage from
Victoria to Skagway.) Several of the ship's passengers were prospectors
who'd struck it rich in the Klondike and were transporting large

quantities of gold south. There were reports of widespread drinking aboard and claims made after the fact that the captain was inebriated. Whatever happened, early in the morning of August 15, as the *Islander* sailed down Stephens Passage, it struck an iceberg or rock. In less than twenty minutes the vessel, crammed to capacity with passengers and cargo (including $6 million of gold in 1901 dollars), sank into the frigid, inky ocean. The mountains of Admiralty Island and Douglas Island loomed silent as the water roiled with chaos.

A few years ago, my little brother, Reid, and I were camped on the backside of Douglas Island near the general vicinity of where the *Islander* went down. We'd spent the day looking for tasty but elusive Sitka black-tailed bucks . . . well, that's not entirely true. Reid shot a nice buck after about ten minutes of hunting and I'd spent the day looking at trees, communing with squirrels, and hoping one would suddenly morph into Bambi's dad. Still, it was a great day. Life doesn't get much better than wandering the woods, having a campfire, and enjoying a clear November night with my brother. We sat in the darkness on a point near the ocean, talking and listening to the sound of waves gently lapping on a tidal flat. Suddenly, I heard voices. We were five miles from the nearest trail or road and it had been dark for hours. Maybe our older brother, Luke, had taken the next day of work off and was hiking out to join us? Odd that he'd be talking to himself though. I shrugged it off. It was probably just some critters or my imagination.

"Did you hear that?" Reid asked. "It sounds like people talking."

We listened and again I heard what sounded like people talking. It appeared they were coming our way. "Yeah, there are people coming. It's weird they can find their way without headlamps. Maybe it's Luke?"

Reid shook his head and I suddenly got the creeps.

Of the 180 or so aboard the *Islander* when it went down, 40 are thought to have died that mid-August morning. *An Inventory of Historic Shipwreck Sites*, a report prepared by the City and Borough of Juneau, Community Development Department in 1992, states, "It was said that a life boat which was designed to hold over forty persons left the ship with only seven survivors in it. Most of the ship's passengers and crew were left to fend for themselves in the frigid waters. Many people drowned as they slipped off makeshift overcrowded rafts, including Captain Foote. Others went down with the ship or were pulled down by suction as the ISLANDER submerged."

Reid and I listened to voices come nearer in the darkness. I fought the urge to put out the fire, grab my rifle, and hide behind a beached log. Instead, we waited and strained our ears trying to make out what our visitors were conversing about. Then, the voices became silent. A few minutes passed. It felt like we were being studied. It might have been irrational, but I wanted to get into the darkness where we weren't illuminated by the fire.

"Well, maybe we should put out this fire and go to bed. Those voices were probably just carrying across the water from somewhere."

"Let's not think about it," Reid said. Our tent was pitched in the cover of an old-growth forest above a small stream. During the daylight, if you look carefully, you can find evidence of an old Tlingit village or camp nearby. We both lay awake for some time, waiting for the rustle of branches, the snap of a twig, or the sound of steps approaching. Right before I was about to punch the clock, an eerie moan-shriek erupted above the tent. It sounded like the song of a porcupine, but I was weirded out enough to not mess with my little brother. The porcupine continued its moan-shrieking long enough for me to climb out of the tent to look for it with a headlamp. It stopped and even though I couldn't find it, I politely asked it to shut the hell up so we could get some sleep. Once I was back in the tent, it started up again.

The *Islander* is best known for its legendary cargo of gold and the herculean effort and hundreds of thousands, if not millions, of dollars salvage companies spent trying to find it. Many of the passengers were rumored to be carrying large amounts of gold. One recovered body was reported to have fifty ounces of gold on it. The dead were mostly forgotten as the imagination of the public and salvage companies turned to thoughts of lost treasure. Dozens of companies tried to penetrate its hull and searched for gold without any luck. In the 1930s a team, using two barges equipped with giant winches and steel cables, inched the *Islander* to the shores of Greens Cove, on Admiralty Island. Once there, according to the City of Juneau and Borough reports, "The ship was literally dug up with shovels and the debris was sluiced. A poke of gold reportedly weighing 17 pounds was found in a washroom. The safe contained between $7,000 and $8,500 in Canadian currency and coins. The salvagers were very close mouthed about what they found. It has been estimated that it cost $200,000 to beach the ISLANDER and that they only got $50,000 for their effort." The *Forest Pride,* one of the barges used to bring the *Islander* ashore, was wrecked in Greens Cove as well.

People are still searching for the *Islander's* lost gold. Its bow broke off in the salvage process and lies decomposing on the ocean floor. Some believe that is where the gold, rumored to be worth between $260 and nearly $800 million in today's market, waits to be found. Ocean Mar, a Seattle-based salvage company, fought a court battle for years over the rights of who owns any potential gold. In 2012 they were granted permission to begin work; the salvage, if fully committed to, could cost "$3 million to $4 million."

Last summer I camped in Greens Cove with ten teenagers and a counselor. I was leading a kayak expedition from Juneau to Pack Creek, Admiralty Island's famous brown bear observatory. I didn't know what I'd signed up for, but quickly realized I was supposed to be in charge of some sort of interpersonal wilderness foray, where victims (kids) are forced to talk about their hearts, souls, and other spooky things. It was raining and the no-see-ums apparently hadn't eaten all summer. My initial relief in getting eleven inexperienced kayakers across Stephens Passage had long since passed. They looked at me with a mixture of disgust and hatred—who was this evil man that led them into this wet and buggy wilderness, and then abandoned them to an equally insane woman who was trying to teach them how to feel? One boy confided in me he'd rather be waterboarded than have to do another trust exercise. I told him never to trust anyone, even himself, and not to worry, life would only get more strange and uncomfortable the older he got.

"You think this is weird? Wait till you get a girlfriend. Man, if I were you I'd run away right now and live with bears," I suggested. He told me he'd miss baseball too much.

In the morning, we walked through the rain to where the *Islander* had been hauled ashore. A giant ship lay in the intertidal zone that was apparently the *Forest Pride*. We walked along the wreckage, hoping for answers but only finding rotting wood and barnacle-encrusted steel. After so many shattered dreams and lives lost, all that remained of the *Islander* was a few rusty steel ribs. Nearby, in a flooded creek, a blue heron hunted baby sculpin and salmon fry.

11.

THE GHOSTS OF THE
HOUSE OF WICKERSHAM

THE House of Wickersham is located on Chicken Ridge beneath the cliffs and slopes of Mount Juneau. The white Victorian house looks down on the bustle of downtown Juneau and the ebb and flow of Gastineau Channel. On the opposite side of Chicken Ridge is Gold Creek, a torrent cascading through a gorge where Joe Juneau and Richard Harris, likely under the guidance of Chief Kowee, made a gold strike in 1880. Several of Juneau's most prominent citizens, including Judge James Wickersham, a frontier judge and politician largely responsible for molding Alaska into a US territory and eventually a state, lived in the house. There have long been rumors it's haunted. Elva Bontrager, who took care of the house for twelve years, knows it is.

"It's a special house," Elva told me when we met for coffee one rainy afternoon. She looked off into space, debating whether or not to say more. "Do I have the right to pass on its ghost stories? Am I telling tales out of school, out of public property, in which I was privileged to live? It might end up being a plus since it would bring people in. I am comfortable with the events I can't explain. That doesn't mean they're unexplainable. Some people consider it so far over the top that they're not comfortable with it."

Judge James Wickersham lived in the house during the last eleven years of his life. He was appointed to serve as US District Court Judge over Alaska in 1900, an honor that likely felt a bit like being sent to the Siberian gulags. Wickersham arrived after the romance and pandemonium of the Klondike gold rush had faded to find men and companies squabbling over mining claims. He was stationed in Eagle, deep in the interior, near the border with Canada. His first case involved the theft of a dog owned by Chief Charley, whom Wickersham said was the leader of the Charley River Band of Tena Indians, by another Athabascan man named "Eagle Jack." Wickersham saw the dog returned to its rightful owner. When he wanted to hold court, Wickersham would slog twenty to thirty-five miles each day on the Yukon River trail to different communities. He traveled almost entirely on foot, frequently through bone-freezing blizzards with the ambient temperature regularly dipping below negative fifty. In Circle City, where Wickersham's brother happened to be serving as the marshal, Judge Wickersham, in his classic book *Old Yukon*, wrote of a note nailed to the jail's door. It read: "All prisoners must report by 9 o'clock pm, or they will be locked out for the night." The cold and isolation kept all but the most desperate of criminals from attempting escape.

During warm months Wickersham traveled by boat, utilizing the Yukon River and its tributaries to settle disputes over mining claims. There were "roadhouses" every twenty to thirty miles, operated by interesting and, generally, friendly folks. However, the owner of the roadhouse that most impressed the judge wasn't hospitable in the least. The story goes that after a long day on the trail, Wickersham arrived at a roadhouse and announced himself.

"'Mr. Webber, I am the United States district judge from Eagle.'

"The landlord's face lighted instantly with a grin, as he replied, 'Oh, the hell you are!' Shocked surprise prevented an answer, and evidently none was expected, nor time given to utter it, for the worthy host quickly continued:

"'Well, this was good country before shyster lawyers and grafting deputy marshals began to come through it with their damned law books and commissioners' warrants, but it's going to hell now as fast as it can go.'"

Wickersham spent a year in Nome, at the time the biggest and most bustling city in Alaska, before moving headquarters to the mining camp Fairbanks in the Tanana Valley. His first case in Fairbanks was brought to him by a horrified Athabascan man who wanted to confess a crime. The man had been hunting moose for a few days when one stepped out and began grazing in a meadow. The hunter dispatched it and approached the "moose" only to find the animal had something seriously wrong with it. It wasn't a moose at all, but "a white man's mule." The judge, believing the man honest, sentenced him not to tell anyone else about the incident.

In 1903, after Wickersham organized the courts and other government offices in Fairbanks, he tore out of town to make the first attempt to climb Mount Denali. The expedition party had no mountaineering experience and, largely due to the stress of wilderness travel, greatly grated on each other's nerves. In hindsight, even though they came nowhere near the summit, the journey was one of the highlights of Wickersham's life. He served seven terms as US District Court Judge, seven terms as nonvoting delegate for Congress and, in the opinion of many historians, was the individual most responsible for building the foundation of what Alaska is today. It was by his efforts and wit that in 1912 Alaska became a US territory complete with its own legislature. Though Alaska became a state two decades after Wickersham passed on in 1939, he was the first to introduce a statehood bill. He was also the impetus behind the Alaska Railroad, the creation of Denali Park, and the University of Alaska. His library was equally impressive—he amassed thousands of books, articles, and diaries on anything Alaskan. According to Terrence Cole, an Alaska historian, "The Wickersham

Library today forms the core of the Alaska State Library's Historical Collection in Juneau."

Elva Bontrager became conscious of a ghost in the House of Wickersham in March of 1989 soon after moving in. She befriended eighty-four-year-old Ruth Allman, the niece of Wickersham. (Allman was equally highly regarded for her famous sourdough starter.) Ruth had been a caregiver to her husband, Jack Allman, who passed on from cancer in the house in 1953. Ruth told Elva that her husband, a writer who worked mostly for newspapers, "didn't believe you should let the truth get in the way of telling a good story." Ruth believed that Jack London had stolen one of her husband's stories and was still irritated by it.

A decade after her husband passed, Grace, the widow of Judge Wickersham, became terminally ill. Ruth cared for her until she passed on. Afterward, she spent much of the rest of her life fighting to preserve the House of Wickersham and share its history. Elva was impressed by Ruth during the six months they got to know each other and become friends. They never discussed anything odd, but Elva quickly realized they weren't alone in the house.

"I would go by the judge's library and every once in a while, not every morning, but often, I'd see a man sitting behind the judge's desk. I'd just kind of smile to myself and in my head, I didn't say it out loud, I'd say something like 'good morning, judge' and go on. I've never had a bad experience. I've never been frightened. Going back further in time, Ruth had only been married once and she was married maybe five years before her husband died of cancer. She was forty-two when they married. He died in the parlor. He was, I think, sixty-two when he died. . . . I was supposed to have tea with her. She called and said she thinks she has the flu. Instead two days later she dies. That was in late September. She died and I never saw that man again. It was like Jack was waiting for her because I never saw him again. I just assumed it would be the judge."

Several weeks later Elva was in the dining room when she became overpowered by the smell of the body wash Ruth once used. After that, she'd frequently but not always catch a whiff of Ruth in the dining room. On December 19, she smelt pine so strongly she figured Ruth was telling her to get her act together and decorate for Christmas. The house was full of odors Elva couldn't explain. She was giving a young woman, who came for a month to volunteer, a tour when they came to Ruth's bedroom.

"Hot dogs and ketchup?" the woman asked as she sniffed in the room.

"I'll explain that later," Elva said, though she had no idea whether or not Ruth enjoyed such a meal while she was living.

Often, when Elva was at the door outside the house, she'd hear people talking, glasses and dishes clinking as if there was a dinner party going on inside. She'd turn the key and open the door to find a silent and empty house. Elva has never seen the ghost of Ruth, though once at the bottom of the stairs she saw a woman in a gray print dress and hair with streaks of gray standing motionless before vanishing. She wonders if it was Grace Wickersham. On another occasion Elva befriended a young actor from England who needed a space to teach a theater class. Elva offered the house and for ten weeks the man taught his class there, which she participated in, once a week. At the end students were asked to write and act out a story or monologue they wrote on their own. Each student performed, until it came to the last person, a reluctant and nervous woman.

"There were times when she would stop and look like she was going to break down and cry," Elva remembered, tearing up herself. "She never did. We were just willing her on. She told this account of a little girl to whom things happened and she really didn't say what these bad things were, but they were bad things. One by one the little girl learned to close that door. Don't think about that. Close this door. Then she said, 'Now this little girl is grown up and she had to open those doors. One by one she has to open those doors and face what's behind them.' It was very moving. At a certain point I saw a man in the doorway to the kitchen and we were in the fireplace room. A man showed up in the doorway and stood there for just an instant and walked straight across and put his arm around her shoulder and stood there for the rest of the account. I never told her. I've thought since I probably should have. I have no idea who it was or what his connection was, or was he simply empathetic. I don't know. He just put his arm around her."

Elva paused and offered me another cup of coffee. I thought of how too often what I remember of history is cruel twists of fate and horrible things we do to other human beings, creatures, and the earth. Elva's stories of the House of Wickersham, with the threads of grace, compassion, and love that connected them all, reminded me of the good in history, and being human. Shortly before we parted, Elva spoke again of the dilemma she felt over sharing her stories of the House of Wickersham.

"I didn't get to know Ruth well enough to know how she'd feel about this, but it doesn't put her down," she said. "In my case, every once in a while, because I'm human, I wonder if this is all there is? I asked my brother, who died and came back, 'Would you rather be here or there?' He smiled and said, 'Would you rather be a baby or an adult?' I don't know exactly what he meant, but I think he was implying we're babies here."

12.

THE CURIOUS CASE OF "THE MOST DIABOLICAL OF ALASKA'S MURDERS"

I N October of 1915, the small boat *Celia* pounded
through the waves of Stephens Passage. The man at the
helm, Ed Krause, a burly shipwright, kept a sharp look out for icebergs
that had drifted in from Holkham Bay and the Taku River. Jagged
mountains rose into slate gray clouds and monstrous glaciers, with
yawning and blue crevasses, manifested out of the sky and stretched
down to the ocean. To the west, termination snow clung to the upper
ramparts of the smaller and heavily forested mountains of Admiralty
Island. The *Celia* passed Grand Island and drew near Taku Harbor and
Doty Cove where Arvid Franzen and his family were homesteading and
fox farming. The journey from Ed's home in Petersburg to Juneau would
have taken more than a day. Perhaps Ed stayed the night with Franzen.
They knew each other and, according to some, were friends. Ed enjoyed
spoiling and playing with children. Franzen had several and their laughter would have lit up the lonely wilderness and acted as a temporary
refuge on the strange and grisly path Ed was traveling.

For being called "Alaska's first serial killer," "a murdering maniac," and "the most diabolical of Alaska's murderers," not much is known about Edward Krause. The only surviving photograph of him is a mug shot in a wanted poster. He looks to be in his forties and has a lantern jaw, a huge mustache, and a cold, mean, calculating glare. The poster reads: "$1,000 Reward is offered for the apprehension of Edward Krause, under the sentence of death for murder, who escaped from the United States jail at Juneau, on the night of April 12, 1917."

Southeast Alaska had its share of frontier violence. Alcohol was a frequent and key component in many of the altercations. Even Soapy Smith, a man who supposedly rarely let booze touch his lips, was drunk the evening he marched to the Juneau Dock to battle it out with Frank Reid and other Skagway vigilantes. The fatal gun battle mythologized Smith and Reid, but the most famous "murderer" in Southeast Alaskan history was Robert Stroud, better known as the Birdman of Alcatraz.

Stroud was born in Seattle in 1890. He came to Alaska in 1907, worked a variety of jobs, thieved, and likely dabbled in prostitution. He was in Juneau during his final months in Alaska, where he was said to have lived with Kitty O'Brien, a woman twice his age, whom he likely pimped for. Stroud was, in his own words, a homosexual and also a proud pederast. The nature of his and O'Brien's relationship and the rationale behind his first murder is a little hazy. What is known is that on January 18, 1909, ten days before Stroud turned nineteen, he walked up to around Fourth Street in downtown Juneau. He entered a shack and shot a man who, according to the coroner, was prostrate in a manner suggesting he was begging for his life. Stroud never revealed the motive behind the killing, though rumors circulated that the man abused Kitty or used her services and refused to pay.

Stroud was sentenced to serve twelve years at McNeil Island Federal Penitentiary. He would have remained a no-name convict, but for reasons unclear, he knifed another prisoner and was transferred to Leavenworth. There he murdered a guard and afterward, in solitary confinement, began his studies of birds and avian diseases. He published a book that convinced much of the public he was a bird expert.

He won further sympathy when Hollywood made the 1962 movie *The Birdman of Alcatraz*, starring Burt Lancaster. He died from natural causes in prison the day before J.F.K. was assassinated. The media had all the right ingredients to make Stroud into a myth of *The Count of Monte Cristo* proportions. His darker elements were overlooked and manipulated into a story about individuality against the machine of society.

But in 1915, when Ed Krause motored the *Celia* into Gastineau Channel, Stroud was forgotten in Juneau and unknown to the rest of the world. The constant pounding of stamp mills crushing ore echoed off the mountains. Ed looked at Treadwell City on Douglas Island with an acute bitterness. The city, along with Juneau and Douglas, was a sort of industrial outpost in which by night, for a few bucks, a man could get drunk and find a woman to satiate an ache. By morning that same man could be hired for a few bucks to work in one of the giant mines, be killed in an accident by the afternoon, dumped in the earth, and forgotten by nightfall. There were always more men, from all over the world, coming into town and desperate for work. Ed had been employed in the Treadwell Mine in 1907 and 1908 and had quickly grown disenchanted with the operation. Yanco Terzich, a miner who worked there during the same time, called the Treadwell Mine "a human slaughterhouse." Ed, a staunch socialist, tried to organize the men into joining the Western Federation of Miners (WFM) union. The union was considered radical and had a reputation for violence. He wasn't the first man to try to get the WFM involved with Treadwell. Every effort before had been squashed by higher-ups in the mine and the Pinkerton Detective Agency. Men who'd signed union petitions were said to have been fired, kicked off Douglas Island, and blacklisted from working in the mines again. In 1907 a thousand Treadwell miners went on strike, their most poignant demands, according to Juneau historian Jack Marshall, being that if they died their families be notified and that they get a funeral complete with a marked grave. Most of the time, new men were shipped in to take the place of those on strike. Terzich recalled how desperate the new men were to work despite the warnings old hands offered: "So one of our men took those men there to the graveyard, and five or six hundred graves, and says, 'You see these graves?'

"They say, 'Yes.'

"'Well, these are all miners killed by the Treadwell mines.'" Many others were buried in unmarked graves. Terzich claimed that only one of two hundred and seventy-five new recruits shown the graveyard joined the union afterward. Ed was fired in 1908 and labeled as a radical socialist. A company-owned union was created, and miners' wages remain fixed until the Treadwell operations ended nearly a decade later. Ed returned to Petersburg, mostly to work as a shipwright, although one account suggests that he tried fox farming, but without success. In 1912, when Alaska became a territory, Krause ran for the territorial legislature on the Socialist Party ticket but failed to be elected.

During that rain-drenched and blustery month of October 1915, perhaps the most depressing time of year in northern Southeast Alaska, William Christie was employed at Treadwell as an amalgamist. It was a valued job, one that involved constant exposure to both toxic mercury and massive quantities of gold. Only a trusted man with a stake in the company would have been allowed to work in such a position. He was also supposedly an officer in the company-owned union. Christie had just married Cecilia Gesekus, a young widow with three children. Her previous husband, John, had been killed in the late summer of 1914, in Oliver Inlet on Admiralty Island, when the hunting rifle he'd been transferring from a dinghy to a cruiser accidentally discharged. He'd fallen into the water, leaving his three companions confused and horrified. They hauled his body, missing the upper portion of his head, out of the water, wrapped him in canvas, waited for slack tide, and returned to Treadwell City with the worst news a young wife and three children could receive.

Some years before the fatal accident, Cecilia had moved with John to Petersburg, where he was able to find work as a carpenter and, likely, on fishing boats. Southeast Alaska was full of unattached men, everything from desperadoes to philosophers, hiding from both real and imagined demons. Ed Krause, overeducated and strangely lonely, seemed more of a ghost than the rest. He showed up in town after losing his job at Treadwell and mostly kept to himself. Those who knew him liked his company for the most part. Erling Strand, in a 1983 article in the *Petersburg Pilot* newspaper, reflected on how much Ed's friendship meant to him when he was a kid. Strand, whose father died in a commercial fishing accident in Norway, came to live with extended family in Petersburg when he was two. Ed Krause was a frequent and welcome visitor in the Strand's home. Erling thought of him as an older brother and treasured memories of Ed teaching him checkers and chess. Ed built Erling a skiff that one day, years later, he would use to transport his own children.

Ed was also a frequent visitor to the Gesekus home, partaking in supper and playing with the couple's children. A bond formed between Cecilia and Ed—they were both born in Germany, and it must have been nice for Cecilia, who likely spoke poor English, to have someone to converse with in her native tongue. Some theorized that Ed was in love with her. Nancy Strand, Erling's daughter, has a memory of hearing that Ed "might have been a bit of a womanizer."

John Gesekus found employment at the Treadwell Mine and left Petersburg for Douglas Island. He didn't bring his wife and children with him, either because he didn't have enough money for a house or because there was a shortage of adequate housing. During his yearlong absence, Ed visited Cecilia and her children frequently. Gerald O. Williams, who served as a district judge in Juneau, wrote that when John found housing "it was Krause who had assisted her (Cecilia) in crating their furniture and packing their household goods." According to Williams, Cecilia later spoke with the authorities about her good-bye with Ed, saying, "He told me how much he was going to miss me and the children, and how he regretted not having married himself." The two stayed in touch by writing letters. Williams wrote, "Finally when her husband, John Gesekus, became jealous of the letters which they were exchanging, she terminated the correspondence." Cecilia claimed she heard no more from Ed, even after she was widowed and would have considered marrying him.

On October 14, a few days before Ed arrived in town, Cecilia and William Christie were married. Shortly after Krause tied up the *Celia*, witnesses at the Treadwell Mine stated he sought out the new husband. Instead of revealing his identity, Ed claimed to be a federal marshal with a court summons for the amalgamist. Christie followed the burly man down to his boat for a ride across the channel to the courthouse in Juneau. A few days later Cecilia received a typed letter claiming to be from William stating he'd been summoned to Seattle for business. The managers of Treadwell believed Christie's disappearance was associated with the Western Federation of Miners and offered a $500 reward for information. It's interesting to consider the reward, which amounts to nearly $12,000 today, juxtaposed with the treatment of most of the hundreds or thousands of men who perished in the mines. Christie was not known to have ever been seen again. During this same time, eyewitnesses claimed Krause engaged in a number of strange activities along Gastineau Channel. His boat was seen anchored in front of Salmon Creek—there's a rumor one man saw him onshore hauling small boulders back to his skiff. Another report stated he was seen with James O. Plunkett, a captain of the charter boat *Lue*, shortly before Plunkett took the *Lue* out of harbor and was never seen again.

A warrant for Ed's arrest was issued and sent all over Southeast Alaska, but by this time Ed was back in Petersburg. Witnesses would later claim they saw a skiff belonging to the *Lue* tied to the dock near Sing Lee's boardinghouse, where Ed took a room. What happened next is a little unclear. One rumor was that US Marshals sent to arrest him let him escape on a steamer heading south. The other story is he boarded a steamer on his own. At a certain point, as the ship passed through the stiff currents and the rain forest archipelago maze, another passenger identified him as the man in a wanted ad. The information was wired ahead and in Seattle the police were waiting to apprehend Krause.

Captain James Tennant, Seattle's chief detective, reportedly found a typewriter, legal papers, and "also several small slips of very light paper containing nothing other than what appeared to be signatures of James O. Plunkett, William Christie, O.E. Moe and K. Yamamoto." Tennant, according to Williams, notified authorities in Juneau with the message that he believed "Krause not only murdered William Christie and James Plunkett, but at least three other men as well."

When the Pinkertons—an extremely powerful and corrupt detective agency zealous in their dislike of labor unions—first took interest in Ed is unclear. The agency had been used by the Treadwell Mine in the past to infiltrate the Western Federation of Miners, and were likely involved in squashing the Treadwell strikes and riots of 1907–8. District Attorney James A. Smiser, according to Williams, contacted the Pinkertons soon after Krause was apprehended in Seattle, and appealed to them to investigate the case. They sent detective F. F. Lischke, a shadowy man who'd been involved in the 1905 Steunenberg trials.

The trials had revolved around the assassination of the former governor of Idaho, Frank Steunenberg, who in 1899 crushed a WFM strike. The Pinkerton's investigation turned into an attack on the WFM. According to many reports, much of the evidence was fabricated and many witnesses had either been coerced or enticed into testifying. Krause, a staunch socialist and a supposed member of the WFM, was exactly the sort of guy the Pinkertons loved to crucify. According to Williams, "The Pinkertons entered the case assuming that Krause, with his known background as a radical socialist, was a hired killer engaged by the violent wing of the labor movement."

Ed was brought back to Juneau in shackles. The *Petersburg Weekly* reported he arrived on the steamer *Humboldt* at the Thane Wharf and was rushed to jail. The article goes on to state, "The prisoner is sullen and defiant. It is evident that he is nearing a breakdown." Ed was quickly tried and convicted of impersonating a federal marshal—stemming from eyewitness accounts of him approaching William Christie with a fake subpoena. With Ed behind bars and in no danger of running off,

Lischke had ample time to build a case with more serious charges. For the next six months the detective unearthed an interesting and damning story. Krause wasn't Ed's real surname—it was Slompke. Before coming to Alaska he'd been in the military and was stationed, among other places, in the Great Plains during the region's last wild days and in Southeast Alaska before anyone had ever heard the word *Klondike*. He was shipped to China to help quell the uprising of the Boxer Rebellion. The strange conflict involved a secret society of mystics who rose to prominence and tried to rid China of Western influences and the exploitation of its people and resources. Ed deserted, which likely led to his changing his name. Lischke believed that while in Chicago, Ed killed and assumed the identity of man with the surname of Krause. He continued his murderous ways, according to the detective, soon after returning to Alaska. Using circumstantial evidence that was quite incriminating, Ed was linked to a whole string of unsolved missing person cases. All involved "single and unattached men" that had disappeared while out in the woods.

Numerous charges were levied at Ed, everything from mail fraud to kidnapping to murder. One by one, he was convicted of every charge. Williams wrote that the prosecution had multitudes of people testify, while the defense had no one, not even Krause, take the stand. When it came time to try Krause for the murder of James Plunkett, he already inspired such angry fervor it was difficult to get unbiased individuals to serve on the jury. It was widely accepted that Ed had not only killed Plunkett and Christie, but at least seven or eight other men. One reporter claimed he killed John Gesekus, Cecilia's first husband. Another writer wrote that he was the leader of a gang of Petersburg goons and had made numerous attempts to murder fox farmers. He was called diabolical. A beast. A demon. Whether or not there's any link, it's also worth remembering that World War I was well into its first year and Germans, like Krause, were not highly looked upon in America. More evidence was presented and the pattern of a serial killer who selected victims without family, enticed them into wilderness, killed them, and then forged legal documents to acquire their assets became apparent. Meanwhile, Ed sat in his chair pale, silent, and hopeless. At times Cecilia watched from the back of the courtroom.

There was no hard evidence that linked Ed to any murders, though. It was all circumstantial. Nonetheless, after six hours of deliberation the jury came back with a guilty verdict for the murder of James Plunkett. Ed came near collapsing. The judge set May 17, 1917, as the day he would hang. He would be the first man to utilize Juneau's gallows since Alaska became a territory. A few years prior another man had been condemned to hang. He was a Japanese cannery foreman named Ido who plunged a sword through a young worker when he complained about having to eat rice all the time and tried to leave. Ido came from a powerful family and they fought a long legal battle that ended up with Ido having his sentence commuted to life in prison.

A month before Ed was to be hung, he escaped from prison. Williams wrote, "On the south side of the main tank, underneath a wash basin, Estes (a jailer) found two bars which had been sawed through and bent out and downwards toward the floor, leaving an 18 inch opening." Apparently Krause had squeezed through the sawed and bent bars, hidden by some toilets, and waited for the jailers to come in to investigate his cell when he didn't answer during roll call. The outside door to the prison was usually locked, but during that fateful moment another jailer, who'd left for a few moments to add coal to the courthouse's furnace, had left it open. Ed Krause, to use the words of one newspaper's headline, "broke jail and escaped into the night." The territorial governor immediately ordered wanted ads distributed posting a reward of $1,000 for Krause, dead or alive. Panic swept through Juneau, Treadwell, and Douglas.

The following morning, more than 1,000 armed men reportedly scoured the woods, beaches, and ocean. This is likely an exaggeration, but still a good indication of the frenzy. At least forty boats cruised the area and formed a blockade of sorts on both sides of Gastineau Channel. Ed had nowhere to go, except, maybe, if he made a twenty-mile trudge through some of the most brutal mountain terrain to the Juneau Icefield. From there, he'd have to trek 150 miles or so across glaciers and the taiga wilderness before reaching the mining camp of Atlin in British Columbia. His chances would have been dicey at best. Otherwise, all routes of escape were seemingly cut off. Notices were sent to Petersburg, Haines, Skagway, Sitka, and Wrangell to keep a lookout. Several communities sent boats to patrol the area.

Arvid Franzen, who had the homestead and fox farm in Doty Cove, was in Juneau working as a boat mechanic at the Thane Wharf when news of Ed's escape reached him. Franzen dropped what he was doing and, according to his later testimony, fearing for the safety of his family, headed to Doty Cove. Interestingly, Franzen also implied he and Ed did not know each other, which is a pretty big contradiction to how Erling Strand remembered things. Not only were the two friends but, according to Erling, Ed had loaned Franzen $1,000 to help his family survive the winter. Franzen hadn't yet paid Krause back.

Ed's escape was baffling. How had he acquired a large knife with a serrated blade while locked up? How had his sawing gone unnoticed by three jailers? Isn't it a bit of a coincidence that the door to the prison was unlocked when the jailers were scratching their heads, looking in Krause's empty cell? How was Ed able to steal an eleven-foot skiff and row out of the narrow and several-mile-long channel and across Stephens Passage to Admiralty Island without being noticed? It seems quite possible Ed had help with his escape. It also seems quite likely that Arvid Franzen may have played a part in Ed's exodus.

The series of events that occurred in the following days only get weirder. Perhaps, as the official story goes, Ed rowed undetected out into Stephens Passage and across to Admiralty Island. Perhaps he hid out in Oliver Inlet in a back slough, haunted by memories of John and Cecilia Gesekus, his guts gnawing with hunger, suffering from the metallic anxiety that comes with knowing you're being hunted. Perhaps, on April 16, he rowed in broad daylight, undetected by the armada searching for him, toward Franzen's homestead. Perhaps, as Arvid

Franzen claimed, at 2:30 in the afternoon a man in a small skiff came onshore and approached his home in Doty Cove. Some accounts have Franzen sending his wife to confront Ed while Franzen hid behind a woodpile with a rifle. The *Petersburg Weekly Report* wrote on April 20, 1917, "Krause approached the rancher's [Franzen's] house from the beach. The rancher secured his gun and met him with the query, 'Are you Krause?' The latter answered 'Yes,' and, according to the testimony before the coroner's jury, turned as if he would attempt to get around the corner of the house. Franzen then shot him twice, one bullet passing through the body near the heart and the other through the head. The rancher also stated that Krause had a bulge under his coat which led him to think he carried a gun."

Perhaps that's how it happened, but it doesn't take an unbiased detective to realize the whole thing smells fishy.

"Franzen made $2,000 in one shot," Erling said. "He didn't have to pay back the loan and he collected a $1,000 reward. But the person government people hated the most was not Krause, it was Franzen. He deprived them the privilege or the pleasure of hanging Krause."

Erling believed Krause was innocent of murder. Other friends of Ed, according to Williams, believed Lischke had concealed evidence that would have been beneficial in Krause's defense. "They insisted that the government officials were apprehensive about the disclosures which the Alaska Socialist Party could make and were using the Krause investigation to cast bad light on the party." On April 17, Ed's body was brought to a coroner in Juneau. The first shot was nonfatal; the other bullet struck Ed in the head and killed him instantly. Arvid Franzen collected his reward. He was exonerated and a hero, at least according to the *Alaska Daily Empire*: "Mr. Franzen will go down in the history of Alaska with Frank H. Reid the slayer of Soapy Smith as a hero in the service of the good name of the Territory and in the interest and respect for the law. Very fortunately, he did not give his own life as an additional price for the service he rendered."

Franzen disappeared from the records after that, except a small notice that he was convicted of perjury, and also that he worked awhile as an informant for a prosecutor after he killed Ed.

Four days later, while the body of Edward Krause lay in the potter's field of Juneau's Evergreen Cemetery, the Treadwell Mine caved in. For nearly a year the mine had been running out of ore. In a final act of greed, miners were directed to "pillar rob"—that is, to drill, blast, and process rock pillars purposely left behind in adits to prevent cave-ins. No metal or wooden support structures were substituted. Tremors, ground settling, and minor cave-ins had become more and more frequent during late March and April. That spring a crack formed in a company swimming pool and bathers barely got out before all the water was sucked out. On April 21, three of the four mines collapsed. Not long after, Treadwell City joined Edward Krause and became a ghost.

13.

THE TRAGEDY OF
THE *PRINCESS SOPHIA*

ILENE Winchell's corpse had been floating in the SS *Princess Sophia* for nine months when it was finally recovered. It was the end of July, at the peak of salmon spawning season, when Southeast Alaska booms with life. Seagulls, with their plaintive and beseeching cries, were gathered around Vanderbilt Reef. Sea lions bellowed across the water from a rookery on Benjamin Island a few miles away. How Ilene's husband, Al, identified her can only be guessed. There was little, if any, resemblance left to the woman he loved. Perhaps Al, after spending eight and a half months and more money than he had to honor a promise he made to his wife, took a second to stare up the rugged fjord toward the end of the Inside Passage. It was time to bring Ilene back to San Francisco to be buried alongside her mother.

The summer before, Ilene had premonitions of her death. Al worked as a miner in Flat, now a ghost town near the western section of the famous Iditarod Trail. In 1910 there had been a gold rush in the area and a number of mining communities had sprung up overnight. At the time the Winchells lived there, Flat likely had a population of several thousand. Regardless of friendships and sources of entertainment, winter, with its darkness and bone-aching cold, was rough for all but the hardiest of individuals. Even though she was only thirty-one, Ilene's health was failing. The couple discussed options and agreed it would be best for her if she went south for the cold months. The thought of the long and arduous journey, combined with her illness, made her nervous and even more fatalistic. Before saying good-bye and boarding a small steamer, she made Al swear if anything happened to her he would bring her body to California.

For the sickly woman, who never felt at home in the northern taiga, the journey was brutal. The Iditarod and Innoko Rivers are small and can't seem to decide which course they want to travel. One disorienting and claustrophobic oxbow after the next greeted the small steamer. At Holy Cross, an Athabascan village and mission, Ilene boarded a larger steamer and motored up the expansive and gray Yukon River. She passed through Native camps and watched people drying salmon, butchering moose, gathering berries, and preparing for the long winter in dozens of other ways. At each village people boarded who, like her, wanted to spend the winter south. The birch, aspen, and willow trees began to turn golden and snow crept down ancient mountains and hills. Rutting moose trolled the riverbanks looking for other moose to fight and mate with. There was something more than a chill in the air, though—Ilene sensed it.

At Fort Yukon, Walter and Frances Harper, a young couple that had just been married by Archdeacon Hudson Stuck, stared at the yellow blaze of birches feeling an overwhelming happiness and sense of possibility. Villagers rushed to say their good-byes before the Harpers boarded a steamer—perhaps the same one Ilene had booked passage on—and began their long journey south to Philadelphia. Walter was born in the eerie expanse of black spruce, birch trees, and tundra of Alaska's Interior in 1893. His first memories were of racks of drying salmon, the buzzing of mosquitoes, the whispering of the Yukon River, the smell of fermenting cranberries, the calls of migratory birds, cold so deep it seemed alive and, most of all, his mother, Seentahna, a Koyukon Athabascan woman. His father, Arthur Harper, dubbed by some the "King of the Klondike," was one of the first white men to come into the north country looking for gold. Walter was the youngest of eight children—and the only one not sent to the Lower 48 to be educated. Arthur, who left the north two years after the boy was born, developed tuberculosis and died just as the great Klondike gold rush was beginning.

Walter was probably born where the Koyukuk and Yukon Rivers meet. His mother's people were said to be starving when his father, traveling with Al Mayo, another pioneering trader of the north, met her on the banks of the Yukon River. Seentahna moved to Tanana soon after the boy's birth. He grew up seeing hunger in emaciated wolves stalking exhausted moose, in flocks of chickadees fighting over the frozen droplets of marten blood, and in the laughter and sorrow of his village. The land, river, animals, and his mother's people were his teachers. When Walter was a teenager he went to an Episcopal boarding school in Nenana. There, he met Hudson Stuck, a most unusual missionary and explorer.

Jan Harper Haines, Walter Harper's great-niece, wrote in *North-field Mount Hermon Magazine*, "According to stories my family told me, Harper was 16 and spoke only his mother's Athabascan language when he met Hudson Stuck, known as the 'Archdeacon of the Yukon.' Impressed with the boy's friendly manner and quick mind, Stuck took on Harper as his dog handler, boat engineer, and interpreter when visiting remote villages in central Alaska. He taught Harper to read and write English, as well as history, arithmetic and geography. After several years of working together, Stuck began envisioning Harper as one who might follow in his footsteps."

Hudson Stuck is famous for leading the first successful ascent of Denali, an expedition that began in March of 1913 by dogsled. On June 7, Walter Harper, at just twenty, became the first person to stand atop the summit of North America's tallest mountain. He was followed by Harry Karstens, Robert G. Tatum, and Stuck, all of whom were weakened to varying degrees. Stuck would later write of Harper, "A native Alaskan, he is the first human being to set foot upon the top of Alaska's great mountain, and he has well earned the lifelong distinction." Stuck, unlike other monomaniacal explorers, by most accounts did not care that much about climbing Denali. His passion was in the taiga, trying to bridge cultures, bringing the word of Christ, and protecting and helping Natives assimilate to the strange, often brutal and predatory nature of colonialism. Harper became more than a companion to Stuck; he became a son, and Stuck's hope for Alaska. After Denali, Stuck sent Harper to a prestigious prep school in Massachusetts. It was Harper's first trip "Outside" into a world that was much more difficult for him to navigate than the northern wilds. Like most obstacles Harper faced, he eventually succeeded. He decided to study medicine. According to Jan Harper Haines, "Stuck, however felt the school's curriculum didn't relate to the young man's future as a missionary, so he decided to take Harper back to Alaska and help him prepare independently for university."

Together, the two set out on a six-month 2,000-plus-mile dogsled journey to different villages and outposts. When they returned to Fort Yukon late in the season, right before breakup, Harper set out alone with a team of nine dogs bound for Circle. The journey was dangerous, but the young man was in love. Frances Wells, who worked as a nurse stationed in Fort Yukon, had been sent to Circle to help fight an epidemic of pneumonia. Walter and his dogs were exhausted when they stumbled into the village. The two were able to spend an evening together before Walter had to make a mad dash back to Fort Yukon. Frances wrote in a letter to her father, "he (Walter) . . . insisting upon it that 'it was worth it' and I don't know but I seconded the motion."

In another letter to her father, written five days later, Frances was giddy and slightly apologetic that her fiancé couldn't ask for his blessing, as she announced her engagement to Walter. She expressed worries about the racism back east that Walter would face. She wrote that she was, "Very well and happier than I have ever been in my life. In fact I have been pretty happy many times but never in a happiest dream did I come to any near what I am these days."

Walter and Frances were married at the beginning of September of 1918, amidst the golden leaves of birch trees strewn around the altar of the Fort Yukon missionary church. Hudson Stuck presided over the ceremony. The lifelong bachelor was likely closer to the groom than anyone else in his life. The newlyweds traveled up the Porcupine River for their honeymoon. They hunted. They listened to silence. They huddled close to each other near campfires. Frances learned to flesh bear hides. Walter might have learned a few new things, too. Frances wrote to Walter's sister, Margaret O'Farrell, on September 28, 1918: "We are just back and have had one famous time—we were gone almost three weeks—our luck was fair, Walter getting two moose, two caribou and three bears beside small game as ducks and porcupine. . . . But it was all miles of fun and I venture to say that no two people could have gotten more real pleasure out of it than we did."

Now, it was time to head south. Frances planned to join the Red Cross. Walter had gotten into medical school in Philadelphia but it also appears, at least according to Frances's letter to her father, the young couple believed there was a decent chance Walter would be shipped out to Europe to fight in the war. Perhaps, Hudson and Walter embraced before the Harpers boarded the steamer *Yukon*. Or, more likely they said their good-byes with the stoicism of people shaped by the wilderness.

Ilene, Walter, and Frances rode up the silty currents of the Yukon River bound for Whitehorse. It would not be long until the river froze and travel would turn to dog mushing, a much more difficult prospect. The last blaze of birches shone golden on the ancient crumbly hills and mountains. Snow was slowly creeping down from the summits and the air bit coldly and smelled of fermenting highbush cranberries. There's no time more beautiful in that country than right before winter, and there was likely no time more beautiful in either Walter or Frances's young lives. As for Ilene, she was no doubt exhausted and couldn't wait to be done with her travels. In Whitehorse, the three boarded the White

Pass Railway and chugged along the hundred miles of rail toward jagged mountains and glaciers. They passed Carcross, near the headwaters of the Yukon River, where Shaaw Tláa, better known in history books as Kate Carmack, lived. A Tagish First Nations woman, she along with her white husband, George Carmack, brother Keish "Skookum Jim," and nephew Káa Goox "Dawson Charlie," discovered the gold in 1896 that set off the Klondike gold rush. The couple worked their claims for a couple seasons, traveled south, and became incredibly rich overnight. Kate experienced a world of excess and racism like she could never have imagined. George deserted her, returned north, fell in love, and married the owner of a brothel. Kate, once deemed the richest Indian woman in the world, now penniless, returned with the aid of her brother to her homeland. She was sixty-one, unhappy and alone, when Ilene, Frances, and Walter passed by. A year and a half later she would die from the Spanish influenza.

The train left Carcross behind and traversed along the mountainsides just above Bennett Lake. Soon the passengers entered a mountainous moonscape. Slate gray clouds and blowing snow engulfed the train at White Pass as it crossed into the maritime environment of the United States. The train clung precariously to cliffs; passengers stared up at mountains so desolate and tall they made them dizzy. The sprawl and bustle of Skagway always comes unexpectedly, like a strange oasis in the wilderness. The small port was alive with the last groups of people trying to flee to southern latitudes. The *Princess Sophia*, a 250-foot passenger liner built just six years prior, was tied to the half-mile-long dock. As latecomers jockeyed for tickets, Ilene, weakened, had to be helped aboard to her cabin.

Ilene, the Harpers, and around 350 other people aboard the *Princess Sophia* departed Skagway late on the 23rd of October, 1918. An Arctic storm howled off the mountains, turning the fjord into a mess of high choppy seas. None aboard were too worried. The *Sophia* was designed for traveling the Inside Passage in all its variances. But the storm combined with a tiny navigational error led the ship to crash atop

Vanderbilt Reef around two in the morning on the twenty-fourth. The radioman sent out a distress call and soon numerous local vessels, mostly fishing boats, braved the storm for a rescue. The captain, an experienced mariner, made the hard decision not to off-load passengers into lifeboats. He hoped the ship would hold fast and the weather would improve, making for a safer rescue.

After forty hours atop Vanderbilt Reef, the rising tide and winds tore the *Sophia* off at around 5:00 P.M. on the 25th of October. The ship went down so quickly it appears there was little time to lower the lifeboats. All aboard, except for a dog, died. Those who were not trapped inside were said to have died mostly from being asphyxiated by tons of gallons of oil that erupted from the torn hull. The tiny communities of Juneau and Douglas sent everyone they had to help, including the territorial governor, Thomas Riggs. The governor was in the chaos of it all, recovering corpses that, as they were covered in oil, reportedly looked more like huge livers than human beings. Riggs worked himself to exhaustion, shock and, perhaps, hypothermia. It was one of the darkest moments in the history of Alaska and the Yukon.

The captain's decision not to off-load passengers has long been questioned. He has been painted as a megalomaniac villain, a coward and drunk womanizer by some. In all likelihood, he was a decent and reliable man presented with a nearly impossible situation. Those aboard the other vessels for the most part remember the weather as terrible. To try to off-load passengers would have been very dangerous, and likely have resulted in deaths.

After he got word of Ilene's death, Al Winchell waited for freeze-up and began his own terrible journey to Vanderbilt Reef. Some accounts say he walked the 400 miles, others say he dog mushed a portion of that distance, to Anchorage, where he caught a steamer to Juneau. On December 21, winter solstice, Al first visited the reef with a diver he'd hired. The Canadian Pacific Railway (CPR), which owned the *Princess Sophia*, had given up looking for bodies. They claimed there were no more to be found in the vessel. Ilene had not been among those who'd been

5

recovered. Al's diver quickly proved the CPR wrong when he found corpses below deck. Over the next several months dive teams brought more and more bodies to the surface. Ilene's pocketbook was reported to have been found in a man's jacket, and her baggage in a different man's room. People gossiped, but Al remained steadfast. He spent all his money paying for divers and then found ways to borrow more. He was reported to have grown old during the months he waited at Vanderbilt Reef, checking each and every grisly corpse that was brought to the surface with the grim hope it was his wife. Finally, in late July, Ilene's body was recovered. Al took her to San Francisco and honored her last wish.

In accordance with Hudson Stuck's request, Walter and Frances were buried side by side in Juneau's Evergreen Cemetery. The taiga was frozen in, and there was no reasonable way to transport or bury bodies north. Their lives were cut short, but their memory remains alive in the savage beauty of Lynn Canal, the towering heights of our continent's biggest mountain, the September glow of the taiga, and the hospitality of the people of the north.

Almost a century after the *Sophia* went down, I floated in a kayak near Vanderbilt Reef. Behind me, the Sentinel Lighthouse shone white in an otherwise gray world. The bellowing of sea lions echoed off a rookery on Benjamin Island and the distant hum of a gillnetter disturbed the quiet of the day. The reef's marker jutted out of the water. When I squinted, I could barely make out surf breaking on rock. The carcass of the *Princess Sophia* is located just sixty feet below the surface, and is now a popular dive sight. Some divers believe it's haunted. Renee Hughes, the caretaker of the Sentinel Lighthouse, has had experiences with the ghosts she believes were passengers on the *Princess Sophia*.

"Out at the lighthouse you occasionally hear people coming up the stairs. You go looking for them and there's nobody there," Renee said. Sometimes, on days when the ocean is calm, she hears people talking nearby even though there are no boats in sight. Things like tools go missing. "The folks from Vanderbilt come visit at the lighthouse. A lot of them, I think, are sad."

The ebbing tide carried me slowly away from the reef, toward Juneau. The sound of a humpback whale breathing echoed across the water. Outdoor recreation is supposed to be fun and light—at least that's how all the models look in REI catalogs—but I felt particularly heavy. I wondered what happened to Al after he made good on his promise. Life is fleeting, but a small rock with an ugly marker in the middle of a savage and beautiful fjord in Southeast Alaska is testament that love is not.

14.

Trouble with Bigfoot

Note to reader: *There are hundreds of names for Bigfoot-like creatures around the world; a few of the more famous include "Yeti" for the Himalayan Mountains and "Sasquatch" for the northwest of North America. For this piece, I'll use the names "Bigfoot" and "Sasquatch" interchangeably.*

MY fascination with Bigfoot began as a child, after I found a copy of the book *Women Who Run with the Wolves*. The cover illustration of a feral woman and a wolf sent shivers down my spine and inspired fantasies ten times better than the stack of *Playboys* my friend's dad left out. I had several colorful nicknames—largely because I entered puberty early and was abnormally hairy and smelly—including "Missing Link," "Ogre," and "Ape-boy." Also, I had an extra set of canines and looked like a bobble-head. This was long before vampires, werewolves, and bobble-heads were sexy and cool. Much of my childhood was spent staring at the cloudy rain forest with an inexplicable desire to be swallowed by it. The way I figured, there was no one besides a woman who ran with wolves who'd ever understand me.

Then I learned about Bigfoot—a lonely, smelly, hairy hominid haunting the edge of civilization. I was smitten, and devoured any literature I could find. There were thousands of stories, everything from tales of trappers being abducted, to sexual encounters with lonely women in their backyards (which was a tremendous relief, as I figured if Bigfoot could get laid I wouldn't die a virgin), to hunters catching a glimpse of something big and hairy in a dark forest. I decided it was time to grow up, put away childish things like fantasies about make-believe wolf-women, and devote my life to cryptozoology (the study and search for animals that by all practical accounts do not exist). Around this time, classmates began calling me "Be-horny." I wasn't sure what horny meant, but my new nickname didn't hurt my feelings as much as the others. During the first day of sixth grade I introduced myself to my art class.

"Hello, my name is Be-horny," I said.

The teacher began to choke in horror and the class exploded with laughter. For a while I was popular. I think I may have had a girlfriend for an hour or two. This facade crumbled when I mentioned something to my new friends about how the cranial capacity of Neanderthals was significantly larger than that of *Homo sapiens*.

"Don't you see? This means Neanderthals had bigger brains than humans!" I said, perhaps a little too excitedly. "And we're about the same size. Some scientists think they communicated telepathically!"

The nicknames came back with a vengeance.

It's also important to note I was tremendously nearsighted. My glasses were perpetually fogged, and did not fit my face. I think I recall the optometrist shaking his head in defeat and mumbling something about my "gorilla skull" during the appointment. I preferred being blind to looking like a special-needs gorilla, so I didn't wear my glasses.

No longer a part of society, I put together a Bigfoot hunting kit consisting of a broken pair of kids' binoculars, a few plastic bags for stool and hair samples, and my Language Arts journal, which doubled as my cryptozoological field book. On my first hunt, I walked to a horse pasture near the Mendenhall Wetlands. Obviously my goal was to find Bigfoot, but I was open to other possibilities. Even seeing a really hairy person would have been exciting. Out near the horse barn, a dark fuzzy blob moved. My heart sung with victory! I looked through my binoculars to make sure. Yep, there was definitely something dark and blurry moving. It looked like it could be between five and ten feet tall and between 200 and 2,000 pounds. All the teasing, confusion, and pain meant nothing now. I had found Bigfoot. *National Geographic* would never believe that an eleven-year-old kid had made the greatest scientific discovery in history. I bagged hair hanging from barbed wire for definitive proof. At home, I wrote in my journal and tried to make a sketch. It looked pretty similar to what I'd seen: a dark blob with some odd equine characteristics.

Despite the fact very few uninhabited and unexplored places now exist, there remains a universal fascination with the idea of a humanlike beast haunting the forest. In Nepal, Tibet, and India, it's the Yeti. In Canada it's the Sasquatch. In Siberia it's the Alma. In most of the western states of the US it's Bigfoot. In Southeast Alaska it's the Kóoshdaa Káa—though there are also reports of Sasquatch. Our obsession with Bigfoot-like creatures, and hunting them, transcends space and time. What's probably the oldest surviving piece of literature, *The Epic of Gilgamesh*, centers around the relationship between Enkidu, a hairy wild man raised by beasts, and Gilgamesh, the king of Uruk. After trying a variety of unsuccessful hunting tactics to capture Enkidu, the wild man is trapped by a woman who literally sexes him into oblivious domestication—an eerie similarity to the lives of many modern men. A reality show on Spike TV offered a "10 Million Dollar Bigfoot Bounty" to anyone able to present evidence the creature exists. A man recently died in Montana after being hit by a car while attempting to enact a Bigfoot hoax.

There's no shortage of people who've gone hunting for Bigfoot. Some go in the hopes of delivering Bigfoot's severed head on a platter to the Smithsonian Museum of Natural History. Others want to find and shelter the cryptid, maybe create a conservancy/amusement park where Bigfoot families can be protected for their own good. Just think of the revenue from ecotourism, not to mention the growth catalyst for all sorts of other avenues of capital gain. North America's most famous hunter was Roger Patterson, a man of questionable repute, who with Bob Gimlin captured the footage of a Bigfoot in 1967. Affectionately known as "Patty" by Bigfoot aficionados, many claim it's a guy in an ape suit while others swear it's the real deal. What irks me the most is the controversy could have been easily solved if the two hunters had the marbles and sense to shoot the damn thing. Even if it was a person it would have been worth it. Patterson and Gimlin were in Humboldt County, famous for its marijuana farms. A maniac wearing an ape suit, out of his mind on weed, would likely rape and murder picnickers and other cryptid hunters. (Just watch *Reefer Madness* for an idea as to what could have happened.) One thing is for certain, after the footage of "Patty" was released, people began seeing Bigfoot all over the country. Since then, there have been plenty of North American Bigfoot hunters, both serious wildlife field biologists and toothless bubbas. They're a colorful bunch, and markedly different from the generally aristocratic yeti hunters of Asia.

The yeti, or the abominable snowman, is thought to be a mostly bipedal, sometimes aggressive, manlike ape of slightly smaller stature than Bigfoot. Many consider it the unsolved riddle of the Himalayan Mountains. With virtually every valley in the Himalayas utilized by people, serious thinkers believe it's increasingly probable the creature exists only in our imaginations. The first supposed documented yeti hunter was Alexander the Great, who went searching for one in the Indus Valley in 326 BC. Some say he even battled a tribe of hairy giants. The first serious attempt in the twentieth century occurred in 1938 when Adolf Hitler sent to the Himalayas an expedition that wanted, among other things, to bag a yeti or two. It was the führer's hope the creature would reveal a direct link between the Aryan race and monkeys. In 1953, Edmund Hillary and Tensing Norgay became the first people to summit Mount Everest. During the climb, the oxygen depleted pair came across what appeared to be the tracks of a huge bipedal apelike creature. Hillary led an expedition in search of the yeti in 1960 without success. He later discounted its existence. In 1986 Reinhold Messner, the great Italian mountaineer and explorer, encountered a strange, seemingly bipedal creature during a 1,200-mile walk across Tibet. At dusk, on a brushy hillside, Messner encountered a large manlike beast that stood upright. At one point the creature was a mere ten feet away. Startled, it ran off into the trees on two legs. Messner happened upon the seemingly angry creature again later that night.

Messner, formerly a skeptic, spent the next twelve years searching for and investigating stories of the elusive cryptid. He came to the unwavering and, to many, disappointing conclusion that what he'd seen, and the yeti altogether, was actually the Tibetan brown bear. Messner later learned that many villagers in eastern Tibet call the Tibetan brown "yeti."

Messner is sure that North America's Bigfoot is the brown bear. Perhaps there's truth to his hypothesis. Awhile back I had a particularly close run-in with a very large bear in the shadowy rain forest of Chichagof Island. I'd been collecting sooty grouse for dinner when, in the gloom of the evening, the bear suddenly stood up from the brush ten feet away. Towering above, it seemed much more than a bear—I would not be surprised if someone in similar circumstances might think they were seeing a Sasquatch, especially if they wanted to. Thankfully, after studying me for a bit, the bear pivoted, fell heavily to the ground, and walked away.

Compared to the rest of the Pacific Northwest, you don't hear about Sasquatch as often in the Inside Passage. Some Southeast old-timers joke that since we have brown bears, we don't need Bigfoot. Most reports of unidentified hairy critters are attributed to the Kóoshdaa Káa, or the Gadiit amongst the Haida on Prince of Wales Island. Said to have once been humans that were lost at sea or to the woods, Kóoshdaa Káa and Gadiits transitioned into hairy, shape-shifting beings that possess supernatural powers. There are more complexities to the Kóoshdaa Káa and Gadiit and it's unclear whether or not these entities belong on the cryptid hit list. At least in the case of the Kóoshdaa Káa, they are more spirit than flesh and hair.

J. Robert Alley, author of *Raincoast Sasquatch*, believes that many Southeast encounters attributed to Kóoshdaa Káas and Gadiits are actually Sasquatches. Alley has collected dozens of stories, stretching from Yakutat south to British Columbia, of creatures who match descriptions of Sasquatch. Almost all encounters are reported to have occurred during twilight, night, and the first light of dawn. This same pattern is true for reports elsewhere in North America. It makes sense that if Sasquatches do exist and their most ideal habitat is the woods of British Columbia and Washington, then some would likely live in Southeast Alaska's colder, more brutal rain forest.

Alley has no doubts as to whether or not Sasquatch exists—he's seen two. The first occurred in 1975 while camped on Vancouver Island. He woke to the sounds of wood knocking and pebbles being thrown onto his tent. Later, he got up to urinate and sensed something watching him nearby from a patch of fireweed. He shone his flashlight on a massive, hairy, bipedal creature towering just a few feet away. The second encounter occurred on the Ketchikan road system in Southeast Alaska when a Sasquatch crossed the road in front of him one evening.

"There's more that's out there than what Western science can put under a microscope," Alley asserted during our phone conversation. "Science is great for the 80 percent of phenomena that are predictable. The 20 percent that's not easy to understand, it fails."

I talked with a woman—who wished to remain anonymous—who believed she saw a Kóoshdaa Káa from her cabin in a remote region of Southeast Alaska between Wrangell and Ketchikan. If she was from British Columbia, Washington, Oregon, or California, she probably would have chalked up the sighting to a Sasquatch, but, like me, she grew up hearing lots of stories of the Kóoshdaa Káa. She related the encounter over e-mail:

I was sitting looking out my cabin window, watching the seagulls playing in the 35mph winds, floating on the winds effortlessly and with the abandon only a bird can do in such weather. The rain was pelting against the window and lending to the gray moodiness that was everywhere that October day. Out of the corner of my eye I suddenly saw a fast/sharp movement and quickly looked to the very edge of the wood-line about 45 feet up on a sheer cliff, just yards from our cabin. I clearly saw a very large grayish mass move quickly and stealthily into the woods, and couldn't for the life of me figure out what I had just seen! I turned to my husband and asked him if he saw what I just did, and he said no. I pointed to the area where I saw the creature vanish into the heavily forested woods and asked, perhaps it was a deer? He explained that the bushes right there were about 6-7 feet tall, so a deer wouldn't be visible, and even a bear on all fours wasn't a possibility, especially not in that area. What I saw was definitely much taller than that as it appeared to be the backside of the creature and it had towered another 5 feet over the bush line, so what could possibly be reaching over 10 feet in height?? My next thought was of course a Kushtaka; based on the many stories I had heard of them growing up, there is no other creature or animal in this part of Southeast Alaska that could account for the size and speed of the creature I saw, cementing in my mind the reality of this elusive creature.

After reading *Raincoast Sasquatch* and digging around the Internet, I was surprised to find reports of Sasquatch encounters on Admiralty Island, Yakobi Island, the Wrangell Narrows, Kupreanof Island, the Malaspina Glaciers, Berners Bay, and Thomas Bay. These were all places I'd spent time exploring, commercial fishing, and guiding. Some of these areas, like Admiralty Island, I'd spent quite a bit of time on. Ketchikan, Alley's hometown, has been a Sasquatch hot spot in recent years. So has Prince of Wales Island. In 2011, there was a flurry on YouTube after someone uploaded a movie purported to show a gray Sasquatch. It's believed by most to be a hoax. I consider myself a pretty decent woodsman, yet, for all I'm conscious of, I've never run across anything Sasquatch.

I did have one odd experience years ago. It was the summer Harrison Ford and Calista Flockhart visited Gustavus for the Fourth of July, causing a mass hysteria in the sleepy gateway community to Glacier Bay National Park. Women fainted. Men stuttered. Children were immaculately conceived. John Lennon or Jesus Christ wouldn't have generated such a ruckus. Even the animals were acting strange. That morning I opened the door to the cabin I was renting, and a panicked Jack Russell terrier dove under the bed. An emaciated wolf, hot on its heels, skidded to a stop just a few feet away. My neighbor popped her head outside and screamed, "OH MY GOD! Did you hear? Harrison Ford and Ally McBeal are in town!"

The wolf stalked away, leaving me contemplating whether *Blade Runner* or *Star Wars* was a better movie. Some questions are too big to be answered, so I grabbed my backpack and set out to escape the parade and festivities. I'd spent the last month on a crab boat trying to learn how to chew tobacco, swear, and look tough—the hardest parts of being a commercial fisherman. Most days had been a bit monotonous, but we had some fun times. A woman at the Excursion Inlet Cannery begged my skipper and me to kill a brown bear that was breaking into buildings and scaring the workers. At Point Adolphus, we responded to a distress call from a sinking boat that had hit a whale. In Port Frederick, a pod of killer whales passed by shortly after a large brown bear trudged across a tidal flat. A couple leapt out of the water in what appeared to be sheer joy. In Icy Strait, the rain stopped and the clouds cleared, revealing alpenglow on the jagged white Fairweather Mountain Range.

I had the Fourth off, so I rode a bicycle to an unmarked trail and followed a small path into the woods that led to a plane crash. The plane went down in 1957, when a C-47 military plane with eleven men aboard crashed while trying to make it to Gustavus. The huge wreck was covered with graffiti and now lies in violent repose. As I sat, the hair on the back of my neck suddenly stood up. I'm woodsy, meaning that some months I communicate more with bears than humans. I don't spook easily and my senses aren't wrong when they tell me I'm not alone. Something was watching, and it didn't feel friendly. I rose and scanned the woods. My unease grew stronger. I tiptoed to one side of the plane and peered around the corner. Maybe it was an agitated bear or wolf or rodent of some sort? Or a squatter suffering from psychosis? I picked up a rock and threw it at a random place. Only silence. Whatever it was, it wanted me gone. I slowly walked back and, there in the middle of the trail I just walked, lay a steaming pile of what looked like, but wasn't quite, human feces. There was no toilet paper and the smell was nearly overwhelming. Who or what deposited the turds did so in plain sight, just a few dozen yards away, while I had my back turned. My Chicken Little screamed at me to run, that there was a Sasquatch or Kóoshdaa Káa watching. I swallowed my panic, did my best to look casual, and even went so far as to "pimp walk" my way out of there. It dawned on me that this style of strutting made it look like I had a broken leg, which might entice an attack. I rode my bike back to town feeling a little less misanthropic and decided going to a barbecue might be fun.

Perhaps I needed guidance and direction. I needed to listen to the master Sasquatch hunters—men and women who call themselves "squatchers"—who've devoted their lives to trying to find and understand the cryptid. I came upon an advertisement for the Sasquatch Summit in Ocean Shores, Washington. The next thing I knew I was sitting on a plane as a three-day blizzard gave up its demons and revealed an expanse of white mountains and black ocean surrounding Juneau. A friend, an emergency room nurse on her way to Haiti to volunteer, sat next to me. It was oddly coincidental, since I was going to the conference with her ex-boyfriend Ben.

"Are you excited to make a trek across the Olympic Mountains?" she asked.

"Oh, hmm. Ah, well, actually, I'm going to a work conference," I said.

"I thought Ben said the two of you were trekking across the Olympics," she said. I could understand how telling your ex-girlfriend that you're going to a Bigfoot conference might be a tad embarrassing.

"Yeah, we're going to a conference on wilderness—sacred headwaters of rivers, yoga and volunteering sort of thing," I said. She totally bought it, but I felt bad and had to tell the truth. This led to two and half hours of yakking about Bigfoot, paranormal experiences, and golden retrievers. In Seattle, I took the light rail and bus to Ben's apartment near the Fremont District. He'd recently moved out of Alaska to attend law school. So far he was enjoying the variety and culture the big city had to offer, but he'd wax nostalgic about the north. We'd covered a lot of miles, often together, through some wild country. Ben was as interested in trying to pick up chicks at the conference as learning about Bigfoot. He'd not bathed for weeks, had only eaten road kill, and had taken to rolling around in dirt and vegetation whenever he had the chance. His theory was that by smelling like Sasquatch he'd become an instant celebrity for the dozens, perhaps hundreds, of young attractive women who'd be attending the conference. He wouldn't even have to talk to them. He could just stand in the corner and grunt as the smell and pheromones lured them in.

The following day we drove through messy traffic on I-5, turned off at Olympia, and headed toward the western shore of the Olympic Peninsula. A flashing billboard advertising the Sasquatch Summit and gambling jutted out of the forest. We turned onto the road to the Quinault Casino. The speed limit was twenty-one and a handful of plywood cutouts of Sasquatches peered out from the edge of the woods. The casino rose above the ocean. Waves were gently crashing on the sandy beach and the sun was setting huge and crimson as people flocked inside to the sound of dinging slot machines. We downed rum and cokes as we waited in a long line of Bigfoot fans, many of whom were bubbling with excitement and talking loudly about conspiracy theories. We were about thirty years younger than most of the crowd. Many folks were knitting. Ben whispered to me that for once in our lives we were in the top one percentile and that as soon as the hot chicks showed up he was going to have to split.

"The government is not your friend," the lady behind us said. "Trust me, I work for the government."

"My husband is here for Bigfoot," the woman in front said, after introducing herself. "He carves Bigfoot statues. For me, it's just a chance to spend the weekend drinking beer and gambling."

We passed vendors selling all sorts of kitschy Sasquatch merchandise and into a huge, almost full auditorium. The first speaker, an erect man with a shiny bald head, wearing a cream-colored sports jacket, stood behind the podium.

"This is scientific research here," he said, and stared out into the audience as if to challenge anyone to contradict him. "Okay? Diagnostic science. Okay?"

His report was on bone piles and bite marks he found somewhere in Washington. It was a little too tame and reasonable for the crowd to get behind. I felt kind of bad for him, but he brought it on himself. Who the hell has such a horrible sense of fashion as to wear a cream-colored suit to present at a Bigfoot conference? And bone piles? I make those in the woods all the time after I kill a deer, tear it limb from limb, and devour its raw flesh. Ben grunted and scanned the room.

"Where are the babes?" he whispered, a sudden look of horror flashing across his face. The second speaker, an older man named Thom Cantrall, asked if there were any skeptics in the audience. No one raised their hand. There's a fine line between being open-minded and being a sucker; my prerogative for the weekend was to keep a low profile and listen. I came back with a couple more whiskey gingers, tripped over all the other glasses that lay scattered around our chairs, and screamed at an old woman who gave me an ugly look.

"When I was young I could whip my weight in wildcats," Cantrall was saying. "Don't get old. It's not worth it."

Cantrall served in the navy for nine years, then earned a degree in forestry engineering and worked for logging operations in Washington and California. He spoke of how roads ruin a place's ecology, and how beautiful the land is. After finding numerous sets of giant tracks while working at logging operations, he became obsessed. Relatively recently, with a companion, he saw two Sasquatches while driving a back road in the dark. All these stories paled in comparison to one night when

Thom was up in the mountains struggling with inner demons. While lying on a cot beneath a tarp, a Sasquatch came out of the darkness and stood over him. Most people would be horrified, but Thom slowly reached up toward the giant. Instead of roaring, attacking, or running off, the Sasquatch gently clasped his hand. Thom expressed worry that if the government ever got involved with Sasquatch, they'd attempt to "manage" the creatures.

"If you put the government in charge of the Sahara Desert, there wouldn't be a speck of sand left in five years," he said, and the crowd had a good chuckle.

He maintains a good relationship with Sasquatches, but never goes looking for them. Instead, he ventures into the woods with a camp chair, a cooler full of Diet Pepsi, and his Kindle. After a few days Sasquatches usually start coming around. He ended his presentation telling the audience that each and every one of us needs to let Bigfoot find us.

"You need to go look in the eyes of Sasquatch," he said with a tinge of sadness.

My mind was blown. I was choking back tears. I hadn't felt this sentimental since the Budweiser commercial about the lost yellow Lab puppy, horse, attractive woman, and handsome man. Bigfoot to Thom was a tale of loneliness, longing, and guilt over the loss of wild areas. A howling eulogy for lost love and ecological emptiness. A barbaric yawp in the face of 10,000 roaring chain saws and 10 million miles of roads. I needed a stiff drink fast, and some chicken wings. The waitress was pretty and friendly and when she said, "Y'all come back again," Ben glowed with success. We drank, gambled, and eventually left the casino pretty sauced to walk the couple miles to where we'd pitched the tent.

At first light, I walked along the misty road, past a great blue heron posted atop a stump in the swamp, to grab Ben's truck. We drove into Ocean Shores for breakfast and missed the Native American blessing that began the conference on Saturday. I later learned it addressed the proper behavior people should have toward Sasquatches, mainly to be respectful and not to try to kill one. I'm sure numerous hopeful hunters got sweaty palms or muttered under their breaths. Many, even the most respected Bigfootologists, believe the only way to ever prove the creature exists is to get a body.

The first speaker was John Bindernagel, BSA, MS, PhD, a wildlife biologist devoted to Bigfoot. Most biologists scoff at the idea of a large primate existing in the ever-shrinking forests, but some, besides Bindernagel, believe it's possible. Jane Goodall, the acclaimed primatologist and saber-tooth hottie who still haunts my dreams, went on record stating she believes in the existence of Sasquatches, or at least wants to. George Schaller, a legendary field biologist, is skeptical but believes Bigfoot is worthy of a more serious study. David Attenborough, naturalist and host of the television series *Planet Earth,* believes Sasquatch-like creatures exist. Ian Redmond, a famous field biologist and primatologist, believes. Bindernagel laid out a general history, including the origin of the creature's name, recorded by British Columbia schoolteacher and Indian agent J. W. Burns in 1920. Burns believed the stories First Nations people told him of the hairy giants, and hoped to encounter one.

A number of other presenters spoke, some pimping their businesses and others showing charts, graphs, and statistics, many of which seemed nonsensical. Then again, math or anything practical was never my strength. One guy from Portland, dressed in a red flannel shirt and wearing a beanie, told the audience he didn't care that much about Bigfoot. What he really cared about was the Bigfoot community. A number of researchers for the Olympic Project presented their data, stating that Sasquatch is as likely to be seen in the suburbs of Seattle as lonely haunts deep in the Cascade Mountains. In fact, there have been quite a few sightings around the Seattle-Tacoma International Airport. The Olympic Project has over 36,000 reports of Sasquatches, most of which were reported occurring near a road during the night. Cindy Dosen told of being stalked by an aggressive, seemingly sexually charged Sasquatch and how that horrible run-in changed her life. Since then, she's been devoted to the cryptid, researching encounters and studying hair samples.

Thom Powell took the stage and told the audience not to buy his books. I whispered to Ben, "By golly, how dare he tell me what to do! I'm going to buy ten copies of each of his books!"

"I'm not even sure if Bigfoot exists," Powell said, after telling the audience he was an eighth-grade astronomy teacher. The guy seemed entirely reasonable; at that point if he'd offered Kool-Aid, I'd probably have drunk it. His first slide showed Bigfoot riding the Loch Ness Monster, illuminated by the light beam of a flying saucer. Ben and I chuckled—this guy had one hell of a sense of humor. Powell defined the paranormal as something you can't study scientifically. "God is paranormal," he said. For the first time ever I wondered if reason and paranormal investigation could go hand in hand. He juxtaposed the skeptic mantra, a quote by Carl Sagan, "Extraordinary claims require extraordinary evidence," to his mantra, a quote by Leslie Kean, "Extraordinary phenomenon demand an extraordinary investigation." I was ready to sign up.

"Fifty years of scientific researched has gotten us nowhere," Powell said, referring to the question of whether or not Bigfoot exists. That's why Powell takes a paranormal approach. He uses a psychic friend to regularly communicate with Sasquatches. He's learned a lot through this technique. Apparently, Sasquatches are not zoologically unverified primates, but rather the foot soldiers for reptilian aliens and belong to the Star Elders cult. Bigfoot call themselves "Nurmana" and their primary purpose is to not be seen by people and to report to the boss aliens what mankind is up to. Bigfoot utilize subterranean habitat; unexplained mounds of earth are evidence. They're also inter-dimensional creatures. If you come across a portal to another dimension in the woods, it's a good idea not to enter it. The crowd loved him. I knew right then and there I needed a psychic in my life.

The next speaker, Ron Moorehead, looked and sounded like Kenny Rogers. He played a recording of weird gibberish, and said that a number of Sasquatches had messed with him and friends in their hunting camp in the Sierras over several decades. His camp was "inaccessible," yet he mentioned a dirt road and how they used horses to travel the eight miles to camp. Moorehead and his friends would "joke around" with the creatures and they were always sober. Joke around with Bigfoot and not drinking while hanging around a hunting camp? These guys sure had an unusual way of getting their kicks. Unexpectedly, a drone flew over the audience and people began getting pissed. A bearded man yelled, "Put it away or get it broke!" I fought the sudden urge to throw my chair or empty cocktail glasses at it. Right when things started to get really ugly, Moorehead yelled over the ruckus for folks to calm down. He'd asked the drone to be flown, apparently to do some filming to have clips put on his website. He resumed his presentation, telling the audience Bigfoot was some sort of extraterrestrial inter-dimensional shape-shifting being. He related a story of his daughter watching one run across a Sierra meadow. By the time it came into view of his granddaughter it had turned into a white wolf. Why a white wolf, I wondered? Why not a gray, black, or brown wolf? Was Bigfoot a racist? Why a wolf at all—why not a gopher or chipmunk? Was Bigfoot species-centric?

There were many other odd occurrences around Moorehead's hunting camp, including orbs of light, humming sounds, metallic sounds, static electricity sounds, knocking sounds, and force fields. One of the more normal things he said connected Bigfoot to the Peruvian Star Children. He spoke a lot about God, stating that "man was made in the image of God and given cognizant intelligence. Bigfoot was given cognizant intelligence but not made in the image of God." This justified humans having dominion over Bigfoot. His last slides showed his fiancée dressed up for a dance when she was sixteen, and then all the different credit cards he accepted for buying his different merchandise. He ended with a list of Bigfoot rules. "Fear is your only enemy. . . . Don't bring dogs. They hate dogs. They'll get eaten. They like the liver."

The next guy called himself a cryptolinguist and based his work off Moorehead's recordings of gibberish. From listening, and downloading a free program with a keyboard on it, he was somehow able to create a Sasquatch phonetic alphabet with thirty-nine letters. He said something about how the creatures spoke an ancient archaic form of Japanese. Then, contradicting himself, he said the gibberish was actually pidgin English. The whole thing got really weird as he imitated 1940s American cartoon characters depicting Japanese nationalists. Maybe Bigfoot is a racist after all.

"Would Sasquatch speak English?" he asked the audience after spouting out a bunch of weird Sasquatch gibberish that was supposed to sound like a samurai. "Yes, of course."

Ben and I left the casino a few hours after sunset, both feeling slightly disturbed. At a gas station, a car with several bullet holes pulled up to the next pump. We sped through the night, past a seemingly endless procession of buildings and vehicles driven by sad, even cadaverous, looking people. The lights of suburbs and Tacoma appeared like an industrial wasteland. A hundred years ago this was all once forest teeming with wildlife and salmon.

According to the Olympic Project, Bigfoot sightings are still being reported in these parts. He's been witnessed dumpster diving and wandering the streets late at night. Some say he helps drunks and junkies home and find a safe place to sleep. Others say he's a murderous rapist and responsible for the disappearance of women and children. Some believe he's Christ, or a cure to their existential voids. A few claim he's their surprisingly gentle and misunderstood lover. A handful of PhDs lie awake each night dreaming of being the one to find him, of that moment of wild intimacy and eternal acclaim that's sure to ensue. Thousands, maybe millions, across North America stare at the woods during weekend picnics, hoping that he's hiding somewhere nearby. The wilderness may be lost, but it doesn't appear Bigfoot is going to stop haunting us anytime soon.

15.

THE WITCHES OF
SOUTHEAST ALASKA

IN the spring of 1957 Ted Reifsteck, an assistant district attorney in Juneau, was sent to the Tlingit village of Angoon to hold a rather strange hearing. A witchcraft craze was taking hold of the Admiralty Island community. It began with the death of a baby and two girls who claimed to turn into cats, cast evil spells on "nonbelievers," and do other magical things. Already on edge, the village was struck with an epidemic of sickness, affecting many people whom the girls claimed to put spells on.

The belief in witches is a worldwide phenomenon, as are witch hunts. Voodoo, an ancient religion often associated with witchcraft, is widely practiced in parts of Africa, the Caribbean, Brazil, and Louisiana. It's the state religion of Benin, a West African nation with a population of more than ten million. Ghana has been trying for years to shut down its "witch camps," where around 1,000 women accused of being witches have been ostracized and forced to live in brutal conditions. In the Philippines, witchcraft is still rampant. A Filipina friend recently told me that her best friend was killed by an angry lover who used black magic. At her funeral, a swarm of flies flew out of her mouth.

Papua New Guinea, famous for its cannibals, also has witches. In the Middle East, the Islamic State has leaked photos of militants beheading several people accused of sorcery. The half-century old practice of Wicca is supposedly one of the fastest growing religions in the US, with between 50,000 and 150,000 adherents. In India, reportedly between 2002 and 2012, more than 2,000 women accused of being witches were tortured and murdered. In 2014, according to the *Washington Post*, Saraswati Devi, a lower caste Indian woman, was dragged out of her house by a mob. It's unclear what her alleged crimes were, other than she'd been accused of being a witch. Two of her sons attempted to intervene but were beaten badly. With the blessing of the local shaman, villagers forced her to consume human feces and beat her to death.

The Tlingit, Haida, and Tsimshian of Southeast Alaska believed in witches as fervently as anyone else. Witches, as across the rest of the world, were believed to cause illness. George Thornton Emmons, a navy man who was stationed in Alaska during the late 1800s, wrote extensively of Tlingit culture. Toward the end of his life, at the request of the American Museum of Natural History, he began organizing decades of ethnographic notes. After his death, Frederica de Laguna, a renowned cultural anthropologist, spent thirty additional years editing Emmons's material before his respected book, *The Tlingit Indians*, was published in 1991. He wrote this about Tlingit belief in witchcraft:

The witch spirit was sought. It was neither born in one, nor came of its own accord [de Laguna believes Emmons may have been incorrect in stating that the witch spirit was always sought]. It was obtained or induced by contact with dead bodies, handling their bones, spending nights around the grave houses, and associating with the spirits that visited thereabouts in the dark. . . . He (the witch) had the power of mesmerizing children and the weak minded. With their assistance, the witch could obtain something bodily from the one to be destroyed: a hair, a nail, or any secretion. This was placed in a crudely made figure like a doll that was put away in the dead body of a person or a dog, usually in the part to be affected. As the doll decayed with the corpse the body of the victim wasted away.

The only chance the bewitched had was enlisting the help of a shaman. Usually a man, but sometimes a woman, shamans held the fabric of society together. By 1957, the tide of Christianity and Western medicine had basically ended shamanism in Southeast Alaska. The witch craze in Angoon was a problem that traditionally was a shaman's job to fix. De Laguna wrote of their cultural importance, "The shaman is the intermediary force between men and the forces of nature. He cures the sick, controls the weather, brings success in war and on the hunt, foretells the future, communicates with colleagues at a distance, receives news about those who are far away, finds and restores to their families those who are lost and captured by the Land Otter Men, reveals and overthrows the fiendish machinations of witches, and makes public demonstrations of his power in many awe-inspiring ways."

When an epidemic broke out, or a higher caste member became ill, a shaman was called to try to root out the source of the disease. If the request was accepted, there was a dramatic ceremony in which the shaman would chant, pray, and call upon the aid of his yeks, or helper spirits. Emmons believed that "the whole cult (of witchcraft) resulted from the shaman's effort to retain his prestige when his incantations failed to save his patient." If the patient failed to get better, the shaman would often accuse someone of being a witch, usually according to Emmons, "someone he hated, that was poor, young, old or a slave." The accused was seized and tortured until they either confessed or died.

The Tlingit shaman had three main opponents—the Kóoshdaa Káa or Land Otter Man, who would steal people; the witch, who would make people sick; and later, Christian missionaries, who were convinced their beliefs and customs were the best way to be human. The clash between cultures was tense, dark, and sometimes violent. Missionaries saw things, such as slavery and persecution of witches, that were difficult for them to stomach. The shamans saw things in white culture, such as the frequent disregard of the earth and animals, and racism, that must have seemed equally mad, brutal, and backward. Since the white man came into the country, there'd been a devastating increase of people dying from illnesses. In some cases entire villages disappeared due to inadvertently introduced plagues. Epidemics of tuberculosis, small pox, and influenza were all believed to be caused by witchcraft.

Widespread belief in witches survived into Southeast Alaska well into the twentieth century. De Laguna wrote that in the 1950s, while there appeared to be no violence against witches in the Yakutat area, many still believed in them. Angoon, in 1957, was the site of the last well-known scare in Southeast Alaska. Authorities in Juneau, knowing Southeast Alaska's violent history of witch hunts, sent Assistant District Attorney Reifsteck, a doctor, and a nurse to the community. A May 3, 1957, article in the *Petersburg Press* stated the following:

> He [Reifsteck] held a hearing at Angoon Saturday. The girl and another girl, 12, each claimed and described their magic powers, but said they could not demonstrate them because it was not midnight. They testified of being turned into cats by a woman they named as a 'witch' and said they saw a woman turned into a cat herself at midnight in the cemetery. A tribal leader said he saw a man turn into a bird and fly away. His investigations, Reifstack [sic] said, convinced him one Angoon family revived the ancient midnight rites after a baby girl's death two weeks ago. At the midnight ceremonies, the girls in turn would name certain 'nonbelievers' and predict certain people would become ill. By coincidence, a virus epidemic broke out and some persons 'named' became sick. The

movement gained followers. However, his investigation and the medical aid being sent to the village should straighten out the situation, he said. [The two girls were taken to Juneau and received by a "home" of some sort.]

About eighty years prior to the Angoon incident, Samuel Hall Young, a vehement Presbyterian missionary, came to Wrangell a few months after the last well-known witch trial conducted by European-Americans occurred in Salem, Massachusetts, in 1878. Salem already bore the weight of America's most famous witch trial, which had occurred some 200 years before. The later case involved two adherents to the new cult of Christian Science. A woman accused a man of exerting mind control over her and causing her health to deteriorate. Although supposedly twenty witnesses testified against the man, the judge dismissed the case, as there was no tangible evidence.

Young was confounded by the persecution of witches he saw in Wrangell. From reading his autobiography, he appeared to have little understanding of the complexities and history of the Tlingits he was sent to convert. His ethnocentrism is apparent with excerpts such as, ". . . we arrived to undertake these ignorant, strange, and very naughty children of the forest and sea from filthy savages to educated and refined Christian citizens." The reverend appeared unaware of the hypocrisy in Christianity's history, such as the Crusades, the Inquisition, anti-Semitism, and the organized persecution and mass murder of ethnic people around the world. I'm not sure if some of his claims were exaggerations, but his account of the witch fever is disturbing to say the least. He described a Mrs. Brown, a Tlingit woman who'd converted to Christianity, who was accused of being a witch and seized. Her husband, a white miner, was away working in the goldfields of the Cassiar region. Four other women who were attending Christian meetings were also accused and seized. One died—Young is not sure whether she was murdered or committed suicide—while the other four women were held in seclusion and tortured to try to attain a confession of guilt.

When Mrs. Brown's husband came home, he cut the women loose, threatened to kill the witch-hunters, and achieved a "... temporary cessation of their persecutions. An old medicine-man who had been a leader in this outrageous torture took to his canoe and fled to distant parts, but there were thirty to forty accused persons, or those who expected to be named as witches, hiding among the islands and up the rivers afraid to come to the town for the fear that they would be seized and meet a like fate. We estimated that during this wave of superstition which swept over the Archipelago that summer of 1878, at least a hundred victims lost their lives, while two or three times that many had been cruelly tortured."

Today, the vast majority of people in the United States believe the idea of witches to be absurd. Most view witch trials as nothing short of an orgy of torture and murder that belongs in the long-ago past. Others will point at McCarthyism, and how it shook the nation in the 1950s, to show that "witch hunts" were part of America at least well into the twentieth century. Americans were accused of being communists instead of witches, but the basic principle of the witch hunt remained the same. Individuals were persecuted irrationally, and frequently with no evidence. The movement preyed upon people's innate fears, and stirred the country to a fever pitch with disturbing similarities to the Salem witch trials of 1692. After the 9/11 attacks, the United States again embarked on a sort of witch hunt, this time for terrorists. The widely used rhetoric had all too familiar echoes of the past.

A real witch, in the traditional sense, seems harder to believe in. Most educated people think the idea is a misogynistic byproduct of our primordial past when we believed, for instance, that people who wear cotton and wool at the same time should, naturally, be stoned to death.

I've only known one person who claimed to be a witch. She was young, kind, and intelligent with nervous quirks. Her life had been rough and confusing—I don't remember her having any real friends. She seemed to suffer from some sort of post-traumatic stress. She was shy, even embarrassed, when she told me. I understood why the idea of witchcraft was appealing. It was a form of empowerment. On another occasion, I half wonder if I ran into a real witch.

It happened during the winter of 2010, while I was biking through the snow-covered mountains of New Mexico during a transcontinental bike ride. In Silver City, at a bike shop, a technician installed tires he claimed could not be popped.

"Short of shooting these with a gun, there's no way you're going to get a flat. They'll definitely get you to the end of your ride," he said. That was saying something, since the end of my ride was the east coast of Florida.

I thanked him and, feeling invincible, headed out into the mountains as a storm was just dying. About twenty miles from the old mining town, on a road with virtually no traffic, a woman appeared in rags, hauling numerous garbage bags and, mostly empty, plastic gallon milk jugs. Instantly, I got the heebie-jeebies. I was speeding down a steep hill and swerved to the other side of the road to get as far away from her as I could. She couldn't see me and was screaming at the top of her lungs.

"I didn't hurt the children!" she yelled, snarling right before I passed. A second later my back tire exploded and I careened to a stop a few yards in front of her.

"Hello, how are you?" I asked, sounding like I belonged on *Leave It to Beaver*. Her face was weathered and her eyes glowed with so much rage and hatred I expected her to come after me.

"He's got a cross to bear!" she screamed, and kept walking down toward a valley.

Do I think she was a witch? Probably not. Note that I said "probably." Albert Einstein famously said, "Coincidence is God's way of staying anonymous." Coincidence sometimes makes me wonder other less pleasant things.

Prior to the Angoon witch scare of 1957, the most famous Southeast Alaska case to make headlines occurred in the village of Killisnoo in 1915. Once located on a small island near Angoon, the village of Killisnoo had a whale and fish reduction plant built on it by the

Northwest Trading Company in the late 1800s. A whaling accident in 1882 that killed a shaman led to a conflict that spiraled out of control and ended in a navy bombardment of Angoon. Many Tlingits remember stories of death that resulted from the razing of the village's storage of food and a lack of adequate shelter for the winter. To this day, many people are still bitter. The Killisnoo reduction plant and village were destroyed by a fire in 1928. The following is from an article printed in the *Harrisburg Telegraph,* a newspaper from Pennsylvania, that tells of the 1915 incident:

> A complaint of the practice of witchcraft among the natives of Killisnoo was made some time ago to W.G. Beattie, superintendent of native schools for Alaska. An investigation in the Killisnoo village led Superintendent Beattie to bring a number of the tribe to Juneau for examination by District Attorney Smiser, with the result the witch was found, but no law was found on which to base a complaint against him.
>
> From the testimony of the witnesses examined before the District Attorney the story of witchery centers around a blind man, his fifteen-year-old daughter and her grandmother. For several months the blind man has been announcing himself as a witch and has claimed responsibility for practically all the deaths that have occurred in the village in the last five years. [The blind man had tried to induct his daughter into witchcraft, but the girl had apparently resisted and appeared most concerned that her dad would kill her grandmother.]
>
> ... The only charges against her father are based upon the firm belief that he is a witch and in that connection he is accused of being responsible for everything in the way of misfortune which has happened in the Killisnoo Indian village. In the eyes of the law, Mr. Smiser says, it does look a little like hypnotism, but nothing tangible has occurred which can be reached by law.

In his remarks before the District Attorney, Superintendent Beattie said: 'The question of witchcraft is one of the most difficult problems we have to handle among the natives. The existence of witches is a certainty with them, and there is absolutely no possibility of convincing them that there are no such things as witches. It isn't stubbornness on their part, it is simply and sincerely their belief that there are among their tribesmen persons who have the power to cast a spell over others of their number.'

The 1957 witch scare in Angoon inspired Helen Moyer Boyd to write "The Witch of Killisnoo," an article about her experiences as a teacher in the village in 1911. Shortly after her arrival on the small island she encountered a small girl named Kitty who, according to Boyd, was a slave and had been hideously crippled by her captors. Kitty was ostracized from the rest of society and forced to haul wood and jugs of water all day. Boyd and the other schoolteacher became more and more disturbed about Kitty's situation. Finally a man revealed to the two teachers that it was widely believed that, "Kitty was a witch—the most vicious witch they had in many years." The girl, maybe ten years old, had been linked to all the misfortune that had occurred in the village. She needed to be killed, but people were afraid of the retribution her evil spirit would likely seek.

One day Kitty vanished. Boyd demanded the child be delivered to her. She even threatened that the US Navy would bombard Killisnoo like it had Angoon unless the people of the town brought the girl to her. People went from house to house screaming and beating on walls with sticks. Boyd wrote: "The noise kept up until all the houses in the village had been well beaten. Then suddenly all was quiet. About twenty minutes later there was a knock on the kitchen door. I opened it, and there stood Kitty. . . . Never before nor since have I seen a human being in such condition. She was filthy from head to foot. Her hair was caked with blood and dirt. Her hands, arms, and legs were lacerated and crusted with blood and dirt. Her bare feet left bloody prints with each step. Her only garment was a thin dress which hung in tatters."

Kitty was left with Boyd and the other teacher after they were warned she'd murder them or turn them into witches and then hurt and kill others. During that night, a number of men returned and demanded Kitty be released. While the other teacher guarded the girl with a rifle, Boyd confronted the crowd of men. "Somehow I mustered the courage I certainly did not feel and said, 'No, Kitty is going away. You can't have her.'" The men eventually retreated back to their homes. The teachers were able to enlist the help of a boat captain, who locked Kitty in the forward cabin until he was able to leave for Sitka. Boyd said it took two months before children began attending school again. She believed the village viewed the two teachers as witch conspirators during the rest of her time in Killisnoo. She transferred to teach at the cannery village of Loring near Ketchikan the following year. The article ends with her thinking of Kitty.

"And what happened to Kitty? Her poor little mutilated body made her slave status plain to the other children at the mission school in Sitka, and in some inexplicable way the stigma of witchcraft went with her. After a few days it was necessary to spirit her away. She was taken to an Indian school in Chemawa, Oregon, and I never heard of her again."

Kitty's legacy lives on in the dark currents of the human soul. Today most people that may have once been labeled as witches are now seen as suffering from some sort of mental disorder. Despite our attempts at compassion, we still don't understand what causes it, or how to fix the torment and madness. We're left trying to navigate the thin line of reason. It's not "witches" we ought to be afraid of, but rather, our propensity toward hysteria and cruelty.

16.

It Came from the Depths: A Brief History of Southeast Alaska's Sea Monsters

WHEN I want real entertainment I walk into a seaside dive bar famous for the different sort of crabs you can get while using its restroom and loudly proclaim, "In the winter of '34 I was rowing across the Gulf of Alaska when a terrible beast reared its serpent head." Usually that gets the pot stirring. After all, nearly every other crusty Southeast Alaskan fisherman has a sea monster story. Some mariner might remark, "Big deal, I've seen several sea serpents. What's the score between the Packers and the Vikings?" Others will start twitching and change the subject to fish prices. If I'm lucky, some peg-legged, one-eyed mariner with three testicles will tell a story so scary it'll turn my whiskers white.

Southeast Alaska is rooted to the mysteries, moods, and whims of the ocean. The greatest event of the year in Juneau is the Golden North Salmon Derby. It's kind of like a mixture of *Mad Max* and Christmas, set on the sea, that includes certain heathen rituals I'm not at liberty to talk about. Southeast kids generally catch their first fish right about the time they learn to walk. Most Saturday night pickup lines end with the simile "like the ocean." Your eyes are like the ocean. Your heart is like the ocean. Your hindquarters are like the ocean—that one gets them every time. Next thing you know, you'll be watching little Ahab roll over and crawl toward a fishing pole. One of my favorite ways to pass an evening is to put on an old halibut jacket, eye patch, and beret covered in fish slime, go to a bar, and tell stories about my past battles with sea monsters.

"Stop talking about your ex-girlfriends," the barkeep eventually says.

"Arr, but she was the size of the *Titanic,* had a head of a goat and eyes like Satan!"

"You sound bitter. Would you like another cosmopolitan?"

"Aye! Did I ever tell you of the time a giant squid was this close to my face?" I'll say, gesturing with my glass and spilling the pink drink on my face.

Being a commercial fisherman impresses many people from the Lower 48. Not so much in Southeast Alaska. At one time or another, the majority of the populace has fished. The job mainly consists of wearing a rubber outfit, smelling rotten, and never changing your underwear. You also have to be able to drink beer, spit tobacco (I prefer grape bubble gum), and every once in a while commit a random act of craziness. Some people attack each other with knives, gaffs, or lead pipes. Others rub against creosote pilings and howl mournfully. I prefer climbing aboard someone else's boat at night and waking them with a good ol'-fashioned tickling. Occasionally, there's fishing involved, an endeavor best described as "wet and messy, a little like sex but generally less pleasurable."

Many outsiders believe fishing is one of the most dangerous jobs in North America. More dangerous than fishing is the drugs fishermen take—they have the constitutions of Charlie Sheen, Sasquatch, and Keith Richards combined. Years ago, I flew out to Elfin Cove to deckhand for Joe and Sandy Craig in Cross Sound, at the northwestern limit of the Inside Passage. The first day, after we set out two longline sets for halibut—a groundline, with a few hundred hooks attached, stretched between two anchors—a friend of theirs showed up with a fresh batch of marijuana cookies. I figured this was some rite-of-passage sort of deal and if I didn't eat one they would call me names and hurt my feelings.

"Wow, very moist! Is it organic? Are these flax seeds?" I asked, as I wolfed one down. No one else partook. Joe and Sandy exchanged concerned looks. An hour later, I sat at the dinner table drooling and unable to speak or move. At 2:30 in the morning it was time to head out and haul in our sets. I was having trouble walking, lifting my arms, and remembering my name. Attempting to urinate was akin to trying to paddle up Niagara Falls. The wind howled off the mountains and the sea was a nasty mess. What ensued was a barbaric ballet of impotency, embarrassment, and shame. For some reason, maybe because I offered comic relief or because Sandy had a history of working with kids with special needs, the Craigs did not fire me or throw me overboard.

Cross Sound has an ancient and enigmatic sense of reality. If there was anywhere in Southeast that seemed to offer a decent chance of encountering a sea monster, it was here, where the Inside Passage ebbs and floods into the big ocean. It took a few seasons before Joe and Sandy opened up with stories, some of which were nothing short of fascinating. Weird stuff happens out there. For instance, one calm morning as we were hauling a longline set, a baby killer whale spyhopped a few feet off the stern and checked us out. I could have reached out and petted the little guy, an urge I had some difficulty quelling.

"It's just a baby orca," Joe said, casting a quick glance. "Let's get back to work."

In Joe's more than forty years of fishing and living in Cross Sound he'd seen no shortage of crazy things. Sandy was the same way. For instance, one night they had a whale get caught in their anchor line and were hauled on a Nantucket sled ride. Joe carefully climbed to the bow and managed to cut the line with his Leatherman. When Sandy was several months pregnant, she was hand trolling by herself and hooked a large salmon shark. The shark began tearing her skiff apart, so she shoved a two-by-four board in its snapping jaws and beat it to death. One evening after a dinner of king salmon and a few beers, Joe casually mentioned he'd come across three different giant squids washed up onshore. They'd been between thirty and forty feet in length and largely decomposed. Sandy had the wildest encounter, a story she didn't tell for years because she was afraid people would think she was crazy. She was hand trolling for cohos near Bird Rock when the ocean began to roil. Suddenly, what looked like a giant snake wreathed out of the water. It undulated through the sea, not showing its head or tail. One coil would disappear under the water and be followed by another. Sandy guessed the creature's sinewy body rose ten feet out of the water and she could have driven her boat through the loop it made. When I suggested that it was a giant squid, she shrugged.

"Maybe, but it seemed too big to be a squid," she said.

Alaska's history of encounters with mysterious sea creatures goes way back. The Tlingit and Haida people, who lived in Southeast Alaska long before the Russians came, knew of several different sea creatures apparently unknown to science. One popular Tlingit story is of a sea monster called Gunakadeit, who brought good luck to a village. Georg Wilhelm Steller, the naturalist aboard Vitus Bering's ship the *St. Peter* during the successful, yet ill-fated, 1741 expedition of "discovery" to Alaska, wrote of seeing a sea ape in the Gulf of Alaska. There was another report of a similar beast around the mid-twentieth century. After the *St. Peter* wrecked and Bering and nearly half the crew perished, the survivors subsisted largely on thirty-foot-long Pacific manatees. The species was rapidly extirpated by Russian fur hunters; its very existence might be questioned if Steller hadn't managed to bring back to St. Petersburg a skeleton of a young female. The Yup'ik and Iñupiat people to the north have stories of sea monsters, too. In the last century there have been hundreds of reports of sea serpents in and near Southeast Alaska—so many that in British Columbia the alleged creature has been given the name of Cadborosaurus, after Cadboro Bay, a hot spot, on southern Vancouver Island. The general description of "Caddy" is a giant sea serpent with a horse-like or camel-like head.

The cadborosaurus cryptid made headlines in 2009 when a fisherman captured less-than-great footage of what he claimed to be a family of sea serpents in the Nushagak Bay region of Bristol Bay. Supposedly there'd been several minutes of footage, but all you can dig up on the Internet is twenty-eight seconds' worth. Two years later, the footage was apparently sold for a handsome sum. Someone filmed a reality television show starring some of the cast from *The Deadliest Catch* as they hunted the sea monster. Bristol Bay is Alaska's biggest commercial salmon fishery; it accounts for nearly half the world's catch of sockeye salmon. When the fish are running strong, the boats of the drift-net fishery are akin to sharks in a feeding frenzy. Boats gouge, ram, and attack. Captains threaten to kill each other's families. The Nushagak is less insane than the Naknek and Egegik districts of Bristol Bay, but still, there is no shortage of boats in the deltas. It's a little surprising no one else came forward to report a sighting of sea serpents. I spent one season in Bristol Bay, mostly because I wanted to see the fishery. People had warned me about the skipper I'd hired on with, but I blew it off, confident that I could charm and get along with just about anyone. The first day the old crust stuck his hand in the anchor winch and exploded a finger. The season ended a month and a half of madness, abuse, and stupidity later when the boat broke down in the middle of the night. Right before we were about to crash into a giant fish packer, the other deckhand, to whom the skipper had been the nastiest, saved us by jimmy-rigging a temporary fix.

One of the earlier recorded stories concerns a group of Haida fishermen from Skidegate, British Columbia, in the Haida Gwaii Archipelago (Queen Charlotte Islands). The *Progressive,* a Petersburg newspaper, related the incident in an article entitled "A Fishy Story" in 1909:

> This creature which appeared to be twenty feet long and from two to three feet in circumference, wrapped itself twice about one of the Indian's paddle. The natives were so alarmed they

dropped paddle and serpent overboard. Next day another party went out and the serpent took a double hitch about the canoe. Then one of the old warriors in the tribe drew forth his keen hunting knife and slashed the monster. It's said of those natives that they are not seriously addicted to fire water and as a general rule, are credited with being quite reliable.

The article's tone might seem dismissive, but the Haida Gwaii Archipelago is, or has recently been, the home to some exceptional beings, including a rain forest caribou, a golden spruce tree, and the Kermode, or spirit bear.

In 1879 Samuel Hall Young, one of the earliest American missionaries to Southeast Alaska, reported being warned of a sea monster. In the company of John Muir, while visiting the Hoonah Tlingit on Chichagof Island, the two explorers asked about Glacier Bay. They were told numerous frightening stories. Young, a skeptic and—I'll venture out on a limb here—opponent of most things Native, blew off the warnings. One creature the Tlingit warned about sounded like a giant squid. "In one bay there was said to be a giant devil-fish with arms as long as a tree, lurking in malignant patience, awaiting the passage that way of an unwary canoe, when up would flash those terrible arms with their thousand suckers and, seizing their prey, would drag down the men to the bottom of the sea, there to be mangled and devoured by the horrid beak."

Forty or so miles west of Hoonah, near Elfin Cove, are the Inian Islands. The passageways between the islands have some of the most powerful currents in the Northwest. Perhaps it's these currents, coupled with proximity to the big ocean, that have led to a number of reports of giant squids washed up on the shore nearby. A couple stories of giant squid attacks circulated among the Cross Sound fishing fleet. One legend has it that a giant monster came into a protected cove where a Tlingit camp or village was situated. Men who were out hunting and fishing returned to find their entire community vanished. From the signs left behind they were able to deduce a giant squid or octopus had attacked. One theory is that children were playing in the shallows when the creature showed up. Mothers and grandmothers ran into the water trying to rescue their children, but were taken as well. The other story was of a giant squid attacking a purse seiner. Sandy Craig told me what she remembered of that tale:

"The way I heard it the purse net was closed and they were bringing the bag up ready to bring the fish onboard. The squid hit the bag at full speed and that is why it was able to pull the boat almost over. I think the boat was a fifty-six-foot limit seiner and it almost capsized. When the force of the initial blow was gone the boat righted itself and some of the crew actually jumped on the bag of fish to cut the squid and they did cut one large leg off."

Another famous story about a different sort of sea monster, one that is well-known to science and quite delicious, is of an old man who was fishing alone when a huge halibut took his bait. The incident was said to have taken place near Kupreanof Island in the early 1970s. The old man brought the leviathan to the surface, gaffed it, and managed to haul it aboard. Later, the skiff was found washed up onshore, with the two lying dead next to each other. In its death throes, the halibut had broken the old man's ribs and legs, perhaps severing an artery. One version of the tale has the halibut being served at the old fisherman's wake. I was a small child when I first heard the story and every time I dropped bait down to the ocean bottom, I prepared to go to war with something akin to Moby Dick. Years later I was longlining with Joe and Sandy when we landed the largest fish I was ever involved in catching. The halibut—we estimated it at around 340 pounds—didn't have much fight when we hauled it to the surface, although getting it aboard took some creative thinking and heavy lifting. According to the *Alaska Dispatch Newspaper* the largest halibut ever caught and weighed in Alaska tipped the scales at 533 pounds. Stories exist of fish brought to the surface and lost that were likely much bigger. Once, in The Office, a bar in Hoonah, I heard whisperings about experienced longliners from Petersburg decades ago hauling a fish to the surface they estimated at around

1,500 pounds. It hovered just off the stern for a few moments before spitting the hook and sinking back into the depths.

Some sea monster tales can be explained with a little bit of research. Teresa Busch, owner of the Plant People in Juneau and a seafaring adventurer, shared a harrowing encounter with one of them. It was after Labor Day, a time of the year when the waters of Southeast Alaska are unpredictable and frequently dangerous. Teresa and her husband, Rick, fell prey to the enticements of a day of calm weather and took their twenty-eight-foot sailboat to go halibut fishing. They crossed Taku Inlet, one of the nastiest bodies of water near Juneau. A lot of mariners have had close calls and many boats have gone down crossing the inlet. That night, while Teresa and her husband were anchored in Doty Cove on Admiralty Island, the weather worsened. In the morning they woke to a gale.

"I almost lost my husband overboard that day," Teresa remembered. Taku Inlet was impassable, but they were able to cross Stephens Passage and tie up to the public float at Taku Harbor. Located twenty miles south of downtown Juneau, Taku Harbor is where the colorful, iconic, and apparently mystical character "Tiger" Olson lived alone for decades. A trapper and prospector who reportedly sometimes communicated with spirits to pass the time, he's become most associated with the harbor. Before Olson, Taku Tlingit families lived in the cove—a census taken in 1880 tallies 269 Taku people living there. In 1840 the Hudson's Bay Company tried to establish a trading post that proved unsuccessful because, according to early traders, the Tlingit were more interested in warring than trading. In the early 1900s a salmon cannery was built. Now the Tlingit villages, the trading post, and the cannery are gone or slowly being reclaimed by the land. A public dock remains, offering many mariners in distress a snug harbor to wait out storms. Teresa checked the weather on the radio; it was supposed to be calmer early and worsen toward late morning. They left in the pitch-black, at three in the morning, to try to beat the storm. Soon the seas were so bad there was no turning back—they were barely able to make it back to Doty Cove.

The following day they tried again. It didn't look too bad from where they were anchored, but when they got farther out the ocean turned into chaos. Teresa estimated the seas running at fifteen feet and the wind blowing sixty-five miles per hour. A giant log popped up in front of the boat. They couldn't back up, so they made a desperate attempt to maneuver around it. They missed the collision by a few feet on their port side. To their horror and fascination, they realized what they thought was a log was a living beast unlike anything they'd ever seen or heard of. It had an enormous head and huge eyes that studied the near-foundering craft.

"It was the most animated I've ever seen my husband," Teresa said. The beast was easily the length of their boat. They passed the creature and it looked back, and then shot straight out of the water and disappeared. Having to focus all their efforts on staying out of the ocean, they had little time to reflect. Eventually, the storm destroyed their boat. A commercial fishing boat picked the couple up and, when the weather calmed down, took them back to town. Teresa approached some Tlingit elders and asked about the beast they encountered and was told it was a creature they knew of that science hadn't identified. Awhile later, Rick came in excited and carrying a magazine with an article about elephant seals.

"This is it!" he said, gesturing at a picture. Scientists have documented elephant seals diving more than 5,000 feet. Teresa believed the contorted features of the creature resulted from pressure changes. Southeast Alaska is not home to elephant seals; however, around the time of Teresa's sighting, a handful of other mariners came upon a large bull elephant seal south of Taku Inlet.

If you fish with someone long enough you get to know them pretty well. Imagine being on a thirty-foot boat for days with someone with a bucket to poop in and only fish, Jiffy peanut butter, and pilot bread to eat. As our friendship progressed, Joe and I both confessed to having what some might see as odd phobias. For Joe it was snakes. The first time we brought a wolf eel aboard, the battle-hardened sea captain screamed and ran for the cabin. Granted, the five-foot-long creature eyed me with an unnerving intelligence. I, on the other hand, only had two phobias: yoga and giant squid. Joe preyed mercilessly upon them both. One spring I talked with him shortly before I set out to kayak around Admiralty Island.

"Kayaking around Admiralty, eh?" Joe said. "There's giant squid out there. A kayaker would be just a piece of popcorn to one of them."

As I paddled out of Auke Bay I could already see the newspaper headline. "Giant Squid Suspected in the Disappearance of Novice Kayaker." According to karma I had it coming. I'd never eaten calamari, but I'd chopped up a lot of little squids for bait. My family and friends were more worried about me getting eaten by a bear (the island supposedly has the densest concentration of brown bears in the world) or caught in stormy seas and drowned. Their concerns were just too damn rational to scare me. The trip was intense in a good sort of way but passed without too much horror. I bobbed around in three-foot seas watching a pod of killer whales attack a humpback whale. When the humpback tried to breathe, the blackfish would push it back under. A week later, in Chatham Strait, I was almost swallowed by the sea during a violent storm that manifested suddenly. Two days before I made it back to Juneau, I had my last adrenaline rush of the trip when a pod of more than thirty killer whales passed by. Three young sea lions had been trailing me for the past hour. With the blackfish approaching, they nervously pressed closer until they were just a few feet away. When sea lions are being hunted by killer whales they'll jump onto anything, dock, buoy, or kayak, in the hopes of escaping. A number of whales approached within twenty yards or so. The sea lions nearly rubbed up against my kayak. One killer whale came toward us, its fin slashing out of the water, before it dove under in what almost seemed like a jest.

I liked to think that Joe was relieved when I showed up on the Elfin Cove floatplane dock a week later. He, Sandy, and I hauled groundlines, anchors, and buoys down to the *Njord*. We drank beer, cut bait, and baited hundreds of hooks. In the predawn darkness, I stood on the dock waiting to untie lines, listening to waves gently lapping and the engine warming up. Joe sat at the helm and Sandy walked down from the house with a mug of tea steaming in her hand.

"Great day!" she said, smiling. She said that almost every morning, no matter what sort of miseries lay ahead. The *Njord* chugged out the narrow entrance to Elfin Cove into Cross Sound. We yelled back and forth while lines and hooks flew overboard as dawn slowly illuminated the Brady Icefield and the massive Fairweather Mountain Range. Humpback whales sounded and a pod of killer whales appeared in the far distance. Afterward, Sandy and I baited hooks in the back of the boat. I took a break to stare out on the ocean. Even if my chances of growing a third testicle were significantly better, I still had hope of encountering a sea monster.

17.

The Haunting of the
Mount Edgecumbe Hospital

I N 1992, Ethel Lund was faced with a rather unusual
problem. The staff of the Mount Edgecumbe Hospital,
which she was in charge of managing, were becoming increasingly
frightened by restless ghosts. Numerous people, from janitors to doc-
tors, reported seeing apparitions or hearing voices and things moving
around in empty rooms.

"I couldn't conceive of seeing a ghost or anything like that. The
doctor said it's beginning to affect our patients because the employees
won't go to certain areas," Ethel said during an interview with Peter
Metcalfe and me. Peter, a historian and author, believes the haunting of
Mount Edgecumbe is "the only ghost story that is not fiction" in Southeast Alaska.

Now eighty-four, Ethel is an icon of the region. If you bring her up
in conversation, you're likely to hear "Ethel is my hero." Before the interview I was warned by one man "to be careful or you might fall in love
with her." Originally from Wrangell, close to where the great Stikine
River empties out into Sumner Strait and Frederick Sound, her Tlingit

name is Aanwoogex' Shtoo.aak and she belongs to the Kiks.ádi Clan (Frog) and Sun House. Her dad, a Swede, died when she was three or four, the result of a fishing accident. When she was fourteen, her mother died from tuberculosis. Her grandparents, Josephine and Thomas Ukas, a famous carver, raised her. After high school, Ethel went to work at the Mount Edgecumbe Hospital, located on Japonski Island, just across a narrow channel of ocean from Sitka. Once part of an army and navy base during World War II, the island's facilities were converted into an Alaska Native hospital, including the largest tuberculosis sanatorium in the territory, and a Native boarding school shortly after the war ended. A lot of people, particularly children, were sent there thousands of miles from their villages and families. At that time, an epidemic of tuberculosis was ravaging Alaska Natives. The villages in the eerie expanse of western Alaska, where the Yukon and Kuskokwim Rivers twist and turn before giving themselves up to the Bering Sea, were the most devastated. Many of the patients had never seen conifer trees, let alone a towering rain forest. Ethel was encouraged to apply to nursing school, but was reluctant because she'd "seen so much death with tuberculosis," particularly with children, at the hospital.

"Most of the children," Peter said, "as far as I know, the children that came from Aleutian villages and Athabascan villages had the type of TB that settled in the bones as opposed to pneumatic or lung TB, which was the most common. They were sent away from their villages, never returned and in many cases there was no report on their death. There was certainly no ceremony. Maybe at bedside or something. I haven't heard anything of that. The fact is, a lot of people died in that hospital and were not taken by their families and buried."

The bodies were interred in places like ammunition bunkers. One such tomb was found in 1998, six years after Ethel organized a ceremony to try to help the spirits of those who died, and those affected by the haunting, find peace. The Associated Press reported in 1998 that 133 bodies of tuberculosis victims were found in a World War II bunker while construction workers were expanding Sitka's airport. The article reported that Bob Sam, a Sitka Tlingit who worked to protect the graves and history of his people, said the discovery brought to the surface years of unresolved grief. Ethel spoke of those difficult times.

"We didn't have the transportation we do now and they died here in our hospital and there was no way to get them home. They had a Quonset hut just off of the community building. They were just piling bodies up in there. They got the records of how many people had passed away and there were over 200."

While tuberculosis has been mostly contained in wealthier countries, it kills 1.5 million people annually. Almost all deaths occur in economically depressed countries. A century ago, and even more recently, it was one of the highest worldwide causes of mortality. Along with other diseases, like smallpox and influenza, Alaska Natives suffered horribly from tuberculosis. Diseases, combined with other negative factors largely due to changes that came with colonization, greatly reduced populations. Ethel is no stranger to the role disease has played in Alaska's history. Not only did she lose her mother young to TB, she was struck by the disease while attending nursing school in Oregon. She'd spend two and half years in a sanatorium, struggling to get out of bed and having lots of conversations with God, before she was cured. Not only did Ethel rise to face the many obstacles life presented, she went on to help found Southeast Alaska Regional Health Consortium (SEARHC). The agency provides medical services and helps countless Southeast Alaska Natives. She served as its first president, and when SEARHC took over Mount Edgecumbe Hospital, Ethel was confronted with a history of grief that needed to be addressed.

It's unclear what year the haunting began. Dee Longenbaugh, owner of Observatory Books, moved to Japonski Island in 1963 when her husband was hired as the chief surgeon at the hospital. Dee remembers using shore boats to travel to and from Sitka—nowadays the O'Connell Bridge provides a way across. She doesn't recall any ghost stories from the hospital. One of her daughters went to third grade in a converted TB ward, complete with dirty old mattresses children would play on. Dee did not find out about the mattresses until years later.

Ethel Lund said it seemed the ghosts were selective about whom they appeared to. I'd heard the same thing from other people who've lived and worked in haunted buildings. That, and sometimes ghosts will stay quiet for an indefinite period of time before something makes them increasingly restless. By 1992, there were unsettling reports from a variety of places in the hospital. Most experiences came from the basement where the mortuary was, and from the floor level the pediatrics unit was on. One story Ethel remembers was told by a friend. The woman was walking through the hallway with her head down when she heard her name being called. She just nodded in a gesture of greeting and passed, but then heard multiple voices calling her name. She stopped and turned left and right, only to find the hallway empty. Another time a janitor came into Ethel's office, which was located on the pediatrics floor, when she was busy working. The man nervously looked all over the place. He asked Ethel if she was okay, to which she answered yes. Later, he'd half explained his strange behavior by telling Ethel that her office was one of the places people regularly had sightings. Ethel isn't aware of encountering any ghosts, but there was one evening when she saw something that gave her pause.

"The only thing—I even question myself—I was driving to the hospital one evening and I was looking at the side of the hospital as I was approaching. On the third floor the window was open and there was somebody leaning out. I thought, gosh, we don't have any patients up there. Anyway, it was all empty. I can't say. It could have been one of our employees," Ethel said.

"I had no idea what to do," Ethel continued. "So, I went to clergy first. Many of our people belonged to the Russian Orthodox Church. I talked with the Russian Orthodox priest and he was agreeable to coming over. He had employees come down to the first floor and preached a short sermon to them and offered prayers. We thought this might do it, but the sightings continued."

What Ethel decided to do next took a tremendous amount of

consideration and courage. She went to different Tlingit leaders and elders, including Paul Jackson, to ask their advice on how to conduct a proper funeral or grieving ceremony. Since many of the patients hadn't been born and raised in Southeast, Ethel knew the ceremony couldn't be Tlingit only.

"We had a challenge to develop a ceremony because of the protocol from the Tlingits," Ethel said. "We had to expand that to include all of the Native groups of Alaska and do it without offending everybody. We really slaved over the ceremony, hoping it would be recognized for what it was: some way to recognize your family or people and release their spirit so they can be free to leave. And also to accommodate any necessary time for grief, and then a time for release of that and a happy time of letting go. We were really challenged because you have Iñupiaq, Athabascan, all of the different groups of Alaska Natives in the state. So we developed the ceremony the best we could."

Ethel wrote to the different villages "and told them many of your loved ones are here." She told them what had happened, how people were interred, and that she was working to create a ceremony "to recognize them." She told them if they could find their way down to Mount Edgecumbe that the Southeast community "would really welcome them." A large number of people came from all over the state and convened at the hospital in June, after herring season. The ceremony began on a beautiful morning. People stood outside watching the sun rise over the jagged mountains of Baranof Island and listening to a drum group from a tribe in Oregon. Eagles began circling and ravens watched with sideways glances from the branches of spruce and hemlock trees.

"Each group had their own, they call them cry songs, songs of grief," Ethel remembered. "They surrounded the hospital—they were standing in groups around—and Paul Jackson was kind of the leader and he would call on different groups and they would sing their song of sorrow. Sometimes it was only two people, but they sang with a lot of emotion. Some groups had a larger number of people. That was so touching. Hearing the drums and hearing the people from different parts of the state stationed around the hospital and singing."

After the drum ceremony, the mourners visited the places they knew had been used as graves. Ethel almost teared up remembering how powerful the experience had been. In the afternoon all the different clan members and many of Mount Edgecumbe's employees were introduced. Ethel, who has worked in health care most of her life, believes in honoring and including employees. The following day at breakfast the ceremony continued with SEARHC board members, who took turns to read the name, tribe, and community of each person who'd died. Some people added the names of people who died more recently. They visited the different floors of the hospital. Each floor had a notebook with the list of names of people who died there. People said prayers and grieved, in their own ways, together.

"Then it came the time for letting go of the grief," Ethel said. "I was just wowed by the immediate change. Paul Jackson, he got everybody telling stories of their lost ones and humorous things. Tlingit humor . . . it's simple stories but they're hilarious. . . . When they announced the tide has come in and that weeping is over, that it's time to have happy memories and happy times. That's when the funny stories come out . . . then dancing and singing. It's just a time of remembering the happy time you shared with that person."

Ethel left for Juneau shortly after the ceremony and when she returned after a brief trip, she swore she could feel a tremendous difference. Before, the building had felt heavy. Now it seemed light. For a while they had a ceremony every year. In time, Ethel and others organized the ceremony to take place in years following Celebration, a biennial festival of Southeast Native cultures. For ten years, Ethel said, there was no talk of ghost sightings. Ethel left her position as board president of SEARHC and no one else took on the responsibility of organizing the grieving ceremony. Soon there were reports the sightings had resumed. Ethel is not sure if these are the ghosts of people who've passed on at the hospital more recently or if it's those who died more than a half century ago. She approached the SEARHC board and told them they need to do a ceremony at least every other year, "but nobody has picked it up. Last year they had fifteen minutes to say a prayer. That was all. Tlingit ceremonies are very intricate and drawn out. You can't do anything in fifteen minutes. So, I feel bad about it. I've gone before the board three times, but nobody's picked it up."

Ethel is still not entirely sure what to make out of the ghost stories, though she also had a few eerie experiences while living next to the Wrangell Institute—a now defunct Native boarding school on Wrangell Island.

"I tend to disbelieve," Ethel said. "But I can't explain how come we're seeing and hearing these things. I still don't know what to make of it. . . . You know for somebody that's been around so long—I'm eighty-four—I can't believe I'm still here. . . . Something happens when a person dies. I can just feel the presence of my grandfather's soul sometimes."

18.

THE GHOSTS OF THE
ALASKAN HOTEL

THE Alaskan Hotel, built in 1913 and deemed "the oldest operating hotel in Alaska," is one of the most popular places to drink in Juneau. Most Friday and Saturday nights, bands, frequently armed with banjos and mandolins, play peppy songs about things like organic farmers accidentally hitting their rescue dogs with trucks that run on waste oil and then having their wives run off with their metrosexual brothers to volunteer teaching yoga in third world countries. The clientele is an eclectic bunch of folks, many of whom work in offices but show up dressed like they've just off-loaded 10,000 pounds of halibut. Ironically, commercial fishermen frequently walk in wearing khakis and looking as clean as hand-polished silver. Conversation varies from typical barroom babble to heated symposiums on jazz, Joni Mitchell's butt, and how different the world would be if Miles Davis had played a cowbell rather than the trumpet. Sure, other bars in Juneau have their perks. The Viking, for instance, has great karaoke and a back room with stripper poles where many inebriated patrons have sustained injuries that shattered their dreams of becoming exotic dancers. Other drinking holes' bathrooms have better cartoon drawings, quotes of barroom wisdom, and hybrid, antibiotic- and kerosene-proof crabs clinging to toilet seats. If you want some real history, walk into the Imperial and sit down for a pint—it's the oldest bar in Juneau. Go to the Triangle Club if you want a quiet, smaller scene with walls of photos of shipwrecks. If you want to get into a knife fight or sell your soul to the devil, go to the Bergman. But, if you're looking for ghosts and scary stories, sidle up to the bar of the Alaskan.

On a blustery winter day, I walked inside the Alaskan Hotel. A man with long graying hair and a handkerchief tied around his neck like a cowboy sat behind the desk. I said hello and asked if he'd had any experiences with ghosts.

"I've worked here for four years and heard the legends, the stories," he said, unfazed, "but haven't had anything happen to me. I attribute that to the fact I'm an insensitive bastard."

He gave me some numbers and e-mails and I walked into the bar for a pint of Alaskan IPA. It was around 2:00 P.M., and the only other patrons were engaged in conversation about global warming and politics, two subject matters that are hard to get away from in Juneau. I stared up at ancient photos of plump prostitutes on the wall—the Alaskan doubled as a whorehouse as late as the 1970s. To this day, it's rumored that on occasion a girl will take out a room and work there independently. Years ago, one night at the Alaskan, one such lady insisted on kissing every male patron. I was the last and tried to put up a fight—Shiva knows how long it had been since she rinsed with Listerine—and the whole affair turned into an embarrassing wrestling match, which she eventually won. I'm socially awkward so I chugged that IPA in less than a minute and then ran from the bar back to my dank hovel, where I felt safe. I e-mailed and called the contacts I'd been given and a few days later Joshua Adams, the son of the current owners, called to have a chat.

"I'm a believer," Joshua said over the phone. "You just don't walk into a place that's haunted and have something happen. You have to have empathy. You have to practice to become sensitive to these things."

He wrote a book on the history of the Alaskan Hotel and is working on another about the hotel's ghost stories. He outlined three types of ghost experiences: obsession, possession, and haunting. From what I could understand, obsession is a place that is cursed generally because something bad happened there. Possession is when a place is inhabited by a spirit that has never lived, something Adams calls an elemental or more earth-based spirit. Haunting applies to the confused spirit of a dead person. Every hospital is full of these type of ghosts, he said.

"The Alaskan Hotel," Joshua said, "has all three types of spirits."

He was surprised when I confessed to having no interest in becoming a medium—I'm already misanthropic enough; the ability to communicate with the dead would only further disenchant me with humanity. Besides, I have no time to cultivate new relationships, especially with entities weighed down with communication issues. I have enough of my own.

A few of Juneau's other hotels, including the Bergman and Silverbow, are rumored to have ghosts. A few years ago my girlfriend, MC, interviewed Ken Alper and Jill Ramiel, who bought the Silverbow in 1997, for an article in the *Capital City Weekly* newspaper. The couple said the hotel "came with a friendly ghost—one generally believed to be Gus Messerschmidt, the bakery's founder." Rumors circulate that maids have experienced less than friendly encounters. Alper said strange occurrences happened most often deep in the night when bakers, often alone, were working in the kitchen. A cart would suddenly roll across the floor, strange sounds would come from the ceiling and once, Alper said, a worker "looked in the mirror and saw Messerschmidt looking back at him." An employee, an Iñupiat man, conducted an exorcism around 2000. According to Alper, "Honestly, after that point we haven't really had any sightings."

Other buildings are said to be haunted in Juneau. I've talked to people who've claimed to see ghosts in the building that once was St. Ann's Hospital and in the older sections of Bartlett Memorial Hospital. While I was growing up, my mom's coworker said her house on Twelfth

Street was haunted. From what I remember, there was something wrong with the basement and a spot on one of the stairs that was always inexplicably wet. While I was researching this book, a number of people mentioned the Twelfth Street house. Local business owner Teresa Busch remembered hearing that a lawyer bought the house but it needed a lot of remodeling. There was one stair he couldn't get a stain out of no matter how much he sanded. During the day he'd work on fixing the place up, but in the evening he ate and slept at another residence. One night he got a call from his would-be neighbors; they told him someone was inside the Twelfth Street house. The lawyer came back and found the neighbors outside, looking through the window. Above the stairs, there appeared to be someone hanging. The man rushed in, but there was no one there.

In Juneau, however, it's at the Alaskan Hotel that things bump the hardest in the night. Many tell stories of a ghost called Alice, who haunts its rooms and hallways. The story goes that she came north with a man, likely a fiancé, and got a room at the Alaskan. He ventured out for a long period of time to look for work, leaving Alice without enough money to pay for room and board. Not knowing what else to do, she turned to prostitution. When the man returned he was heartbroken; it's unclear if he murdered Alice, if she killed herself, of if she was murdered by another lover.

Teresa Busch had a pretty typical Alice sighting in the early 1990s. She was staying at the hotel when she left her room, accompanied by her boyfriend, to use the shared bathroom. Down the hallway stood a woman dressed in an elaborate old-time saloon outfit. The woman was acting strange and appeared to want her attention. Teresa continued a few steps toward the bathroom before, feeling uneasy, she looked back at the woman. She was no longer there and it didn't seem there was anyplace she could have gone except into the wall.

Elva Bontrager, while having coffee with an acquaintance shortly after she arrived in town in the late 1980s, had an odd experience in the Alaskan. She was on her way to use the restroom when she was struck by a painting of two women. One was a tall, scantily-clad, sour-faced blond. The other was an attractive dark-haired woman with a small scar on her cheek, sitting behind a small green table. Elva assumed the two were prostitutes; she went home and replicated the painting of the two women. She asked other people about the portrait, but nobody knew what she was talking about. A couple weeks later she returned to the bar with an acquaintance, who in the past had worked at the hotel as a maid. The painting was gone. The entire restroom had become more modernized, too.

"This acquaintance said, 'I think you should stop talking about it,'" Elva recalled. "I said, 'Why?' She said, 'I can't tell you how often I've heard that blond described.' One of the things people had told her and the house [staff] is that this tall blond would go down the hall in front of them and, turning the corner, would go straight on. She also said room 321 was impossible to keep clean."

According to Joshua Adams, the Alaskan has tried exorcisms and brought in priests, but the ghosts are still there. Several people have killed themselves in the hotel. Adams remembered one guy who, not that long ago, phoned his girlfriend and asked her to come to his room, where she found him dead next to a note that read "I have a gift for you."

Another of the Alaskan's stories, Joshua said, is about a fisherman whose girlfriend was staying in room 315. The man, suspicious his girlfriend might be cheating on him, desperately wanted to come into port. It was autumn, a time storms frequently buffet Juneau and turn the ocean deadly. Rather than staying anchored in a protected cove, the fisherman made a run for town and was lost to the stormy sea. Staff and guests hear a fisherman's steps walking up the stairs during the first big storm each year.

One night a guy, who Joshua thought might have been in the military, came in drunk and asked to stay in a haunted room. He was let into 315. Soon, there was yelling and a commotion. According to Joshua, the police officer first on the scene was horrified from what he heard and, perhaps saw, from the other side of the door. Before the officer could talk down or restrain him, the guest leapt through a window. To this day, the officer won't talk to Joshua about it, he said.

He's not sure whether or not the man died, but believes he at least broke his neck. He also believed the incident was covered up because the man was in the military. The room was covered in blood when Joshua and other staff were allowed in to clean.

The most creepy ghost, according to Joshua, belongs to a man who drowned in a hot tub in the basement. Joshua will never forget that night—he ran downstairs and pulled a large, overweight man out of their biggest hot tub. The man was dead, but Joshua began CPR anyway. He speculated the man, shortly before he died, may have been robbed of a big cash dividend a Native corporation had recently paid. Now, he said, there's a poltergeist that can be aggressive, particularly to women, in the basement—though they don't offer hot tubs anymore.

The Alaskan Hotel, for better or worse, is alive with memories. It's a place so full of nostalgia it'll make your skin crawl. It's also a good place to wet your throat, gawk at attractive weirdos, and get a sense of at least one facet of Juneau culture. You can take comfort that even if you go in by yourself, there's a good chance you won't be drinking alone.

19

NAKED JOE: ALASKA'S

MOST FAMOUS AND

LEAST KNOWN GHOST

A LASKA'S most famous haunting is the ghost of an alcoholic, pudgy nudist named Joseph Knowles. Very few Alaskans know of him, though his influence is felt far and wide. His ghost has colored much of the world's perspective on what Alaska is like. In his youth, Joe was muscular, handsome, and possessed a piercing dark gaze. He was probably quite the ladies' man, hot-rodding around with horse and wagon, and hand-holding and necking if he got lucky. This was the 1890s in America, long before the automobile and Elvis created sex.

In 1913, Joe, now a sad, middle-aged newspaper illustrator living in Boston, left a throng of reporters and ventured into the Maine woods wearing only a jockstrap. He claimed he would survive naked and alone in the wild, relying solely on his wits. (Well, almost naked. One can't blame him for taking preventive measures against testicular torsion.) Joe, even with balls intact, was destined to be as alone as the last wolf watching the Great Plains eaten up by cattle, oil rigs, and strip malls. I don't blame Joe for wanting to be naked in the woods—my mom always said, "Let he who hasn't woken up naked, covered in blood and dung, in the ditch next to a murdered cow cast the first stone."

During the two months Knowles spent alone in Maine's wilderness, the *Boston Post* regularly published notes and drawings he made with charcoal and the bark from birch trees. He emerged from the forest a national celebrity, wearing clothing fashioned from the skin of a bear he said he clubbed to death.

Nearly a hundred years later, I stood in a meadow on Chichagof Island watching the antics of an Alaskan reality television film crew. I was hired as a guide and packer for the shoot. We'd been in country renowned for its density of brown bears for two hours when the producer approached me.

"We really need to get an aggressive bear encounter on camera. What are the chances we can make that happen?" he asked me. I was a little confused as to why anyone would want to have an aggressive encounter with a bear, let alone film it—I was young and my heart was an open book.

"None," I said.

"I really need it, though," he said. For a few moments there was a heavy silence as we plodded up a muddy slough crisscrossed with bear tracks. Snowcapped mountains rose from each side, a bald eagle circled high above, and a raven croaked from deep in the forest. One of the "contestants" was a tall, skinny guy from back East who billed himself as the fittest man on earth. The other two were Alaskans, one a famous dog musher and the other an Iñupiat oil worker. Two cameramen set up to film the three surviving in the wilderness. The producer laid out his plans for the next shoot.

"Let's end this scene pretending to be attacked by a bear," he said. The three contestants huddled up and brainstormed. Who would take lead? Which way should they run? Or should they walk? How did their hair look? Do these Patagonia pants make their hips look big? While they debated their roles, I thought of a friend, a commercial fisherman, who used to homestead nearby. Five years previously, after a day of mending crab pots, I borrowed his skiff to visit this same meadow.

"It has the most beautiful wildflowers," his wife exclaimed.

I putted up the inlet in pouring rain, around a few sea otters as a young chocolate-colored brown bear eating grass ran into the rain forest. Four bears were said to have been recently killed by guided hunters in the inlet and the season was still open.

The meadow was quiet, the wildflowers still at least a week away from blooming. I didn't mind though—it was nice to be alone with the ocean and the forest. Harbor seals surrounded the boat as I drifted with the tide and watched smoke-colored clouds swirl over the dark green mountains. Late in the evening, a gigantic boar, looking more like a draft horse than a bear, emerged and began grazing. I left the skiff tied to a rock and, though it was foolish and disrespectful, approached unarmed on foot. Between mouthfuls of grass, the bear watched indifferently as I came closer. Guilt slowly tainted the electricity thrumming through me. Did the monarch know the difference between me and the members of Cabelas' army that wanted his hide stretched across their living room walls? He lifted his barrel-sized head and stared at me and I believe he did. I retreated to the skiff and left the bear to his solitude. When I got back to the cabin and out of my rubber rain gear, my friend sat me down.

"Don't move!" he commanded, his voice hoarse from years of smoking and yelling at inept deckhands like me. He disappeared into the kitchen where I heard whispering and giggling, then popped out with his wife and another crusty fisherman in tow.

"This is what we did when we were your age, before television took over the world!" he said. Together they counted to three, then sang and danced the hokey-pokey. A year later my friend passed on to better fishing grounds. Shortly thereafter television sort of did take over the world, or at least the world's perspective on Alaska. Like an oil boom or gold rush, a wave of film crews flooded the north to exploit the idea of the last frontier and its wilderness. They depicted everything from Sarah Palin blasting away at a young caribou, to survivalists almost dying in the wilderness, to gourmands cooking Alaskan cuisine, to strange-looking bearded men hunting Bigfoot. While I write this, *Deadliest Catch* is broadcast in three-quarters of the world's countries. I didn't know what reality TV was the night my friends danced the hokey-pokey. Since then, I can't keep track of all the different film crews I've blundered into. The "set" I currently stood on didn't differ much from experiences I'd had with others.

"Bear! Bear! Bear!" the fittest man on earth yelled and began running away as a cameraman chased after him. The two Alaskans trailed behind looking a little sheepish. At least they were being paid good money.

"Are you supposed to run from a bear? No? Okay! We need to shoot the scene again! This time slowly walk away!" the producer hollered. I couldn't help but think of all the bears in the forest watching and listening to us play pretend in their home.

Over the next few days, the cast was confronted by "aggressive bears" in a variety of habitats and scenarios. Most encounters had to be filmed a couple times. Dramatic music, crackling brush, grunting, maybe roaring and actual footage of bears could be added later in the production process. Would the narrator mention that nearly one out of fifteen of Alaska's estimated 32,000 brown bears are shot annually by trophy hunters? Would he mention that until August of 2012, Alaska had gone seven years without a fatal mauling? Somehow, as I watched the cast pretending to almost die in a variety of scenarios, then drug squirrels so they could pretend to snare and then eat them, I doubted it.

A hundred years ago, shortly after Joe Knowles claimed to conquer the wilderness naked, the veracity of his story was disputed. After filing a lawsuit, he hauled a small captive black bear into the woods. In front of witnesses, he bludgeoned the docile animal to death with a club to prove his prowess. After a book, a stint on the vaudeville circuit, and a Hollywood movie, Joe slipped into obscurity. Nearly twenty-five years after he walked into the woods his claim was proven to be a hoax, not that many cared anymore. Joe's ghost haunts Alaska to this day. Just turn on your television. Chances are you won't have to change many channels before you'll see him.

20.

Juneau's

Front Street Ghosts

I T was a dark and stormy November morning. I had errands to run before I headed downtown to interview "Jane," an employee at Juneau Drug Co., about the store's basement being haunted by an angry ghost. At the grocery store I carried a half dozen energy drinks, five bunches of organic kale, and a thirty-pound bag of dog food to the self-checkout line. The numbers 666 kept appearing when I tried entering the kale's bar code. The night before a strange black dog kept barking at my door. He liked my golden retriever puppy Fenrir okay, but freaked out when I tried to grab his collar to look for his owner's phone number. Naturally, I was a bit on edge as I drove downtown, wondering if Satan was really as bad as all the stories made him out to be. Gastineau Channel was frothing with whitecaps and snow on Douglas Island was nearing sea level. I was beginning to wonder if the *Haunted Inside Passage* book was a bad idea. Perhaps I was messing with something that wanted to be left alone. I so did not want to be that guy in the movie *Paranormal Activity*. If Fenrir barked "redrum" I vowed to abolish the contract I had with my publisher, lie on the couch, and watch episodes of *The Office* all day.

"Guard the car, rascal," I told Fenrir. Near where I parked, a gated gravel road stretched down the back of the Valentine Building. "Welcome To Hell" was painted above the door. This was all getting to be too much. Fenrir stared at me with doe eyes that seemed to say, "Daddy, what will we eat? How will we survive the cold, wet winter? Daddy, please write the book? Please write the book?"

Darn it, for you, Fenrir, I would.

I avoided eye contact with sodden looking people who appeared heavy with thought and tinged with melancholy. It's the Juneau look that time of the year. One man, dressed like Max from *Where the Wild Things Are*, latched onto me. It's one of my favorite books, but this guy appeared to be in his sixties. He wore a tan wolf pelt. The beast's head acted as a hood and its tail hung down from the man's backside. He carried a candy-cane staff and wore knee-high leather boots with bells that jingled with every step he took. He gestured into the Rookery Cafe.

"A lot of pretty girls in there," he said, then looked to me for agreement. What is it about me that makes creepy men want to penis bond? Do I look like a rapist or give off a molester vibe? Was candy-cane wolfman another sign I should call off all this spook research? I made a neutral grunt that sounded a bit like a spaced-out bull caribou shortly after it's finished mating. It's one of the passwords of the penis fraternity. Candy-cane wolfman jangled on up the street with a smile on his face. He was proof that ghosts, aliens, a fifty-foot-tall young Daryl Hannah, and even finding and teaching the Blair Witch how to love, stop abducting children, and become a good churchgoing mother but freak in the bedroom were possible.

Trying to collect myself before going into the Juneau Drug Company for the interview, I stared in the window's reflection of Shoefly (a fancy shoe store) and did mouth exercises. It wasn't supposed to open for another half hour so I was safe to express myself.

"Brown cow now. Now brown cow. Cow now brown. Diddly do dop bop licky bum lee." A lady inside the shop appeared and stared at me with a mixture of confusion and fear. I looked up, like I'd been admiring the architecture of the Valentine Building. After all, it was quite impressive, especially considering it was built in 1912 by a one-legged miner named Emory Valentine. Emory hailed from Michigan and, at the age of ten, headed west to work in the mines of Colorado. In the golden state he lost a leg in a mining accident. Survival deemed he learn a new trade, and his ingenuity led him to become a jeweler, architect, real estate mogul, politician, and firefighter. He's said to have arrived in Juneau in May of 1886, bought a plot of land from Joe Juneau, and promptly set up shop. Soon he had a variety of businesses and owned quite a few properties. His accomplishments were many, but I'll list just a few. He created the Juneau Volunteer Fire Department and built the Juneau Dock in Skagway, which a short time later gave Frank Reid and Soapy Smith adequate space to kill each other during their legendary gunfight. He served as Juneau's mayor for six terms, was married three or four times, and died of stomach cancer in 1930 in his apartment on the upper level of the Valentine Building.

The day before I talked to Jane of Juneau Drug Co.—located in the front of the Valentine Building—I told her I was working on a book of scary stories and unsolved mysteries of Southeast Alaska. To my surprise she did not laugh when I asked about the basement.

"I've been working here for twenty years and never had anything directly happen to me, but there are a lot of stories. Come on over. I'll take you down to the basement, turn off the lights, and you can do whatever you like."

Her offer was more generous than I expected and I knew it would be foolish not to take advantage of it. I drew a deep breath, opened the door, and proceeded to make a neighing sound at the girl at the front counter—I always make barnyard animal sounds when I'm nervous. Soon I found Jane. She's the kind of person who exudes friendliness and makes socially awkward people like me feel at ease. She'd heard numerous stories from other employees, mostly female, who felt like they were stalked by a malicious, unseen male presence while they were in the basement. Some men have had experiences too, including objects flying off shelves. Many began refusing to go to the basement when asked to grab merchandise to stock the shelves. One said she frequently felt something breathing on her neck when she was down there. Jane did some research and her sources led her to believe the basement might have been used as a morgue for the bodies recovered from a shipwreck. The story she heard is that nearly 200 corpses were recovered after a horrific accident, brought to Juneau, and stored until they could be identified and shipped to appropriate burial grounds. Most of the victims had died from being covered and asphyxiated by the thousands of gallons of oil the ship gushed out as it sank. There was a building across the street that was used for storage of corpses, but there was an overflow. The basement was used to store the excess. Jane's story sounded a lot like the sinking of the *Princess Sophia,* the biggest maritime disaster in Southeast Alaska probably ever, which occurred six years after the Valentine Building was constructed.

"There's also a story of a man falling down the stairs," Jane said. She wasn't sure which, or if either, were true. She led me down into the basement and showed me the part they called the dungeon. The lights wouldn't turn on, so I shined a headlamp. It was dank and creepy. A staircase led into a bricked-off wall. I'm going with a psychosomatic explanation, but a wave of nausea settled heavily on me.

A few years ago, when work was being done on the basement's sprinkler system and boiler, the ghost became particularly active. It got so bad that a number of employees were too scared to do their jobs properly.

"It was a big ordeal two years ago. The girls were dead serious. The one felt she was being harassed by it. She said I'm not going back down there. I was like fine, we're going to turn the lights off and we're calling this thing out. This is ridiculous, you have to do your job," Jane said, glancing over her shoulder, as she led me down the stairs. "The other girls turned off the lights, sat in a circle, and the next thing I know they were screaming. One said somebody touched her back. The girl sitting next to her said, 'I Did Not Touch Your Back.' One of the girls went into the boiler room and sat down. She started screaming and begged us to turn on the lights. She said something darker than the darkness was right in front of her face."

They left the basement worse for wear. Jane didn't notice anything too strange during their attempt at holding a séance, but an odd sound did make her a little uneasy. I followed her back to the stairs; she paused and looked through me and into the basement's gloom.

"I thought the girls were just being stupid and didn't want to work down here," she said, and then proceeded to tell me a story that made her believe something really was going on. Jane called her friend Teresa Busch, someone she considered level-headed and intelligent, yet sensitive to the spiritual world. The two walked down the stairs but Teresa wouldn't take a step past the last stair.

"She stood right here and froze. I looked back and she was in tears. She said there was something angry down here. He's mad. I said, 'All right, let's go back upstairs!'"

Jane and I returned to the first floor and said our good-byes.

I called Teresa Busch on the phone for an interview. She doesn't believe what's haunting the basement of Juneau Drug has anything but the worst intentions.

"That ghost has history," she said, a trace of fear audible in her voice. This wasn't her first encounter with a spirit. When she was a child her family bought an old house in need of remodeling. While her dad fixed up the bedrooms, she and her siblings camped out in the living room. The first sign something was amiss was when the family woke one morning to find that all the windows and doors of the house had been opened. Everyone in the family began to have experiences with something that seemed friendly but, at times, mischievous. Whatever it was, it seemed most interested in Teresa. Once, after a weekend outing the family returned home to find all the windows and doors open. Cautiously, they walked inside. Flour and baby powder had been flung everywhere and images of houses had been drawn in the resulting mess. Not long after, they found out a little girl had died from appendicitis in the house a few years before they had moved in.

The ghost in Juneau Drug's basement was unlike anything Teresa had encountered. Jane had called and asked her to come by, without fully explaining what was going on. Halfway down the stairs, Teresa suddenly had trouble breathing and she felt it.

"It was such a depressing feeling. It felt like someone really wanting to hurt you," Teresa said.

Slowly, she continued to the bottom of the stairs. Jane was in the lead and already walking toward the part of the basement called the dungeon. Teresa froze; she couldn't breathe and was shaking uncontrollably. There was something evil in the darkness watching her.

"It wasn't angry that it died. I felt like the thing just wanted to hurt you," Teresa said.

She wanted to run, but she could barely move, let alone climb the stairs. Tears streamed down her face but she doesn't think her crying was inspired from any normal emotion. The best way to describe it was like a really extreme case of being outside on a cold day and having your eyes water. Jane, sensing her friend's distress, helped her up the stairs. Afterward, Teresa dug into historical archives and is convinced that some of the bodies from the *Princess Sophia* had been stored in the basement. She also believes a murder occurred in Skagway or Yukon shortly before the *Princess Sophia* set sail to its doom. Teresa wonders if the murderer stowed away and it was his ghost she encountered. One thing is for certain—she'll never to go into the Juneau Drug's basement again.

Up Seward Street, the owner of Lisa Davidson's Boutique, also in the Valentine Building, laughed when I asked her about ghosts. She hadn't experienced anything personally, but shared the story she'd heard. It was short and to the point. Emory Valentine left the building to one of his business partners when he died. The second owner died after falling down the stairs into the boiler room and it's his ghost that haunts the building.

"Supposedly, he looks after the place," Lisa said, with a slight smile.

I thanked Lisa and stepped back out in the rain. I was loosened up enough to go investigate another ghost story, this one at Annie Kaill's, a fine arts gallery. Annie Kaill's is just about the last place on earth you'd expect to be haunted. It's the sort of store a man goes to shop when he's made a mess with his lady. Maybe he misspelled her name in an anniversary card after being together for several years. Maybe, after a great night out with the guys, he came home and mistook her dresser for a urinal. Maybe instead of going with her to visit her family, he went to a Bigfoot conference. When a ten-dollar bouquet of flowers and chocolate won't remedy relationship strife, Juneau men in the know go to Annie Kaill's. The store is stocked with original works that make you look like you're really thoughtful and spent a lot of time picking out a gift. I stood outside the shop feeling weird because I hadn't done anything wrong. At least, I thought I hadn't. You can never be too sure. The store was empty except for a young woman at the counter. She looked over nervously as I nearly stumbled into a display and then stammered:

"Hi my name is Bjorn Dihle I'm writing a book on unsolved mysteries and scary stories of Southeast Alaska I heard you had a ghost I was wondering if you'd be willing to talk with me about it hi my name is Bjorn Dihle I'm writing a book on unsolved mysteries," I said in one breath, sweating profusely.

"What? A ghost?" she asked, quailing. Had my informant, JD, a seemingly nice but overly existential young man, led me on? Had I teased him too much about being angsty? Was he getting back at me for saying I found Dostoyevsky's last novel, *The Brothers Karamazov*, tedious, unimaginative, and one of his worst works? He had the three Karamazov brothers tattooed on his bicep—which, I admit, is one of the coolest ideas behind a tattoo, akin to having "Drake" permanently inked on your face. The girl stared at me with a mixture of horror, fascination, and confusion. JD had set me up. Vengeance would be mine. I was just about to storm out, track him down, and administer my specific set of skills, including interpersonal sock puppetry, to let him know he kind of hurt my feelings, when the girl smiled wistfully.

"Oh, you mean Hector," she said. She'd recently begun working at the gallery and had only heard stories. A number of employees had experiences, but Hector seemed most interested in a young woman who no longer worked for the gallery. He was thought to be the ghost of a Hispanic construction worker.

"He's a friendly ghost. He'd help her out. Like bring her a stapler when she needed one," the girl said and then added a little sadly, "I guess he just doesn't want anything to do with me."

She was new to town and originally from Alabama. New arrivals often find Juneau a hard place to make friends. It's largely due to the weather; there's something about the slate gray clouds and rain that makes many residents extra introverted. Knowing how difficult an adjustment Southeast can be, I make a point of inviting out new folks and giving them a good old-fashioned hazing to see whether or not they're friend material. This normally involves a mountain goat, a bottle of grain alcohol, and my imaginary pal, Long John Silver. For a second I wondered if I should extend an invitation to the girl. Long John Silver was in prison for something involving a mountain goat, grain alcohol, and some guy new to town. Soon we were swapping stories about how charged and haunted the South is. It's funny how sharing ghost stories is a bit like going to a bar on Sunday to watch football with strangers. You find yourself arm in arm, hooting, hollering, crying, and screeching. By the end of our conversation I wanted to tell the girl that Hector was a fool not to haunt her, but I thought that might come across a little weird.

"You really remind me of my mom," I said instead. "She's really cool. She taught me sock puppetry."

Outside, homeless folks in a variety of states of inebriation and psychosis stood and sat under the building's dripping awnings. People with places to go hurried past. We all avoided eye contact. Maybe it was just the gloom of the November afternoon or a bad batch of hallucinogenics I took when I was fourteen, but all of us on Front Street seemed more ghost than living.

Sources

Abercrombie, William Ralph. *Alaska. 1899. Copper River Exploring Expedition.* US Government Printing Office, 1900.

Adams, Joshua. *The Life and Times of the Alaskan Hotel.* 2nd Edition. Self-published.

Alley, Robert. J. *Raincoast Sasquatch.* Surrey, BC: Hancock House Publishers, 2003.

The Associated Press. "Bodies identified from Sitka bunker." *Juneau Empire,* January 26, 2000.

The Associated Press. "Remains of tuberculosis victims heading home from Sitka: State paying for return of bodies kept in bunker in World War II." *Juneau Empire,* July 10, 2000.

Babyak, Jolene. *Bird Man: The Many Faces of Robert Stroud.* Oakland, CA: Ariel Vamp Press, 1994.

Baker, Bruce. "The Sinking of the Steamship the *Islander.*" Friends of Admiralty.org. www.friendsofadmiralty.org/steamship.html.

Beck, Mary Giraudo. *Shamans and Kushtakas: North Coast Tales of the Supernatural.* Portland, OR: Alaska Northwest Books, 1992.

Berton, Pierre. *The Klondike Fever.* New York: Alfred A. Knopf, 1974.

Boyd, Helen Moyer. "The Witch of Killisnoo," *The Alaska Sportsman,* Volume XXIV, Number 3 (March, 1958).

Campbell, Robert. *In Darkest Alaska: Travel and Empire Along the Inside Passage.* Philadelphia: University of Pennsylvania Press, 2007.

Carroll, Tony. "Channel skull find rekindles discussion of local legend: Whether it was death by squid or scuba accident, some say bone fragments are George Tonsgard's." *Juneau Empire,* March 8, 2004.

Coates, Ken, and Bill Morrison. *The Sinking of the Princess Sophia: Taking the North Down with Her.* Fairbanks: University of Alaska Press, 1993.

Colp, Harry D. *The Strangest Story Ever Told.* Petersburg, AK: Sing Lee Alley Books, 1994.

Dauenhauer, Nora Marks, Richard Dauenhauer, and Lydia T. Black. *Anóoshi Lingít Aaní Ká: Russians in Tlingit America: The Battles of Sitka 1802 and 1804.* Seattle: University of Washington Press, 2008.

De Armond, R. N. *The Founding of Juneau.* Olney Printing, 1967.

Emmons, George Thornton. *The Tlingit Indians.* Seattle: University of Washington Press, 1991.

Engstrom, Elton, and Allan Engstrom. *Alexander Baranov: A Pacific Empire.* Juneau, AK: Self-published, 2004.

Frost, O. W. *Bering and Chirikov: The American Voyages and Their Impact.* Anchorage, AK: The Alaska Historical Society, 1992.

Gibbs, James A. *Sentinels of the North Pacific: The Story of the Pacific Coast Lighthouses and Lightships.* Whitefish, MT: Literary Licensing, LLC, 2013.

Harper-Haines, Jan. *Cold River Spirits.* Kenmore, WA: Epicenter Press, 2000.

Heaton, John W. *Outlaw Tales of Alaska: True Stories of the Last Frontier's Most Infamous Crooks, Culprits, and Cutthroats.* Rowman & Littlefield, 2015.

"Inventory and Survey of Historic Shipwrecks Sites." Juneau, AK: City and Borough of Juneau, Community Development Department, 1992.

Laguna, Frederica de. *Under Mount Saint Elias. The History and Culture of the Yakutat Tlingit.* City of Washington: Smithsonian Institution Press, 1972.

LeBlond, Paul H., and Edward L. Bousfield. *Cadborosaurus: Survivor from the Deep.* Victoria, BC: Horsdal & Schubart Publishers Ltd, 1995.

Levi, Steven C. *The Clara Nevada: Gold, Greed, Murder and Alaska's Inside Passage.* Charleston, SC: The History Press, 2011.

Martin, Mary Catharine. "Ghosts of Southeast Alaska." *Capital City Weekly,* October 30, 2013.

McCoy, Terrence. "Thousands of women, accused of sorcery, tortured and executed in Indian witch hunts." The *Washington Post*, July 21, 2014.

Messinger, Nick. "The SS *Islander* Story." Nick Messinger's Home Page. www.nickmessinger.co.uk/islander.html.

Messner, Reinhold. *My Quest for the Yeti: Confronting the Himalayas' Deepest Mystery*. New York: St. Martin's Press, 2001.

Neilson, Tara. "The Rest of the Strangest Story Ever Told." *Alaska for Real by A Daughter of the Walrus*. September 17, 2015. www.alaskaforreal.com/blog/category/monster-busting.

———. "Legends of the Kushtaka." *Alaska for Real by A Daughter of the Walrus*. September 17, 2015. www.alaskaforreal.com/blog/kushtaka.

———. "Kushtaka Conclusions: First Contact." *Alaska for Real by A Daughter of the Walrus*. September 15, 2015. www.alaskaforreal.com/blog/kushtaka-conclusions-first-contact.

Norton, L. M. *Boston Alaskan: Published in the Interest of Alaska*. Boston, MA: Boston-Alaskan Society, 1906-1907.

O'Neill, John M. (editor). *Official Proceedings of the Twentieth Annual Convention: Western Federation of Miners*. Denver, CO: Great Western Publishing Co, 1912.

Rasmussen, Frederick N. "Descendants offer stories from ill-fated *Clara Nevada*." The *Baltimore Sun*, June 18, 2011.

Redman, Earl. *The Juneau Gold Belt: A History of the Mines and Miners*. Anchorage, AK: Publication Consultants, 2011.

Saunders, Aaron. *Stranded: Alaska's Worst Maritime Disaster Nearly Happened Twice*. Toronto, ON: Dundurn Press, 2015.

Smith, Jeff. *Alias Soapy Smith: The Life and Death of a Scoundrel: The Biography of Jefferson Randolph Smith II*. Juneau, AK: Klondike Research, 2009.

Spring, Norma. "Gold rush trails: Visitors strike it rich in tourist attractions along Yukon route." *Chicago Tribune*, March, 1978.

Spude, Holder Catherine. *That Fiend in Hell: Soapy Smith in Legend*. Norman: University of Oklahoma Press, 2012.

Swagel, Will. "Sitka event recounts history of TB in Alaska." *Capital City Weekly*, March 24, 2010.

Thomson, Lori. "SE's most mysterious residents: Tales of kushtakas linger long after sightings." Petersburg, AK: Viking Visitor Guide, 1994.

Tichenor, Katy. "Citizens' labor built first plank streets in Petersburg." *Petersburg Pilot*, October 27, 1983.

Turner, Wallace. "TB Remains a Stubborn Foe for Alaska." The *New York Times*, July 3, 1983.

Williams, Gerald O. "Alaska Killer: the enigma of Edward Krause." Papers. Alaska State Archives.

———. *Alaska State Troopers: 50 Years of History*. Alaska: Alaska State Troopers Golden Anniversary Committee, 1991.

Woolsey, Robert. "Original Brave Gil Truitt '48 shares Mt. Edgecumbe History." KCAW (Raven Radio) November 20, 2012.

Victor-How, Ann-Marie. *Feeding the Ancestors.* Cambridge, MA: Harvard University Press, 2007.

Young, Samuel Hall. *Hall Young of Alaska: An Autobiography.* New York: Fleming H. Revell Company, 1927.

Anonymous. "Death of Krause." *Petersburg Weekly Report*, April 20, 1917.

———. "Duck-Father Takes Girl Ride: Tells Strange Story in Court of Witchcraft Practice in Alaska." *Harrisburg Telegraph*, November 11, 1915.

———. "A 'Fishy' Story." The *Progressive*, September 20, 1913.

———. "Krause Breaks Jail and Escapes In Darkness." *Petersburg Weekly Report*, April 13, 1917.

———. "Krause Fights Extradition." *Petersburg Weekly Report*, November 20, 1915.

———. "Krause Indicted For Murder." *Petersburg Weekly Report*, May 6, 1916.

———. "No 'dwarf' expedition ever arrived at Thomas Bay in Aug." *Petersburg Pilot*, November 29, 1978.

———. "Other Murders Are Recalled by Nelson Charles Case in Ketchikan." *Petersburg Press*, April 28, 1939.

———. "Prospectors in Petersburg visit 'Devil's Country.'" The *Petersburg Press*, September 9, 1932.

———. "Strange Legends Established Early in This Area." The *Petersburg Press*, March 22, 1957.

———. "Thomas Bay expedition is termed foolish." *Petersburg Pilot*, December 13, 1978.

———. "Witchcraft Practices Ends." The *Petersburg Press*, May 3, 1957.